Reaching out
to the child

Reaching out
to the child

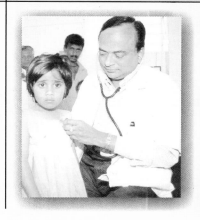

An Integrated
Approach to
Child Development

Human Development Sector
South Asia Region
September 2004

OXFORD
UNIVERSITY PRESS

THE WORLD BANK

OXFORD
UNIVERSITY PRESS

YMCA Library Building, Jai Singh Road, New Delhi 110 001

Oxford University Press is a department of the University of Oxford.
It furthers the University's objective of excellence in research, scholarship,
and education by publishing worldwide in

Oxford   New York
Cape Town   Dar es Salaam   Hong Kong   Karachi   Kuala Lumpur   Madrid
Melbourne   Mexico   Nairobi   New Delhi   Toronto   Shanghai

With offices in
Argentina   Austria   Brazil   Chile   Czech Republic   Eire   France   Greece
Guatemala and Central America   Hungary   Italy   Japan   Korea   New Zealand
Poland   Portugal   Singapore   Switzerland   Taiwan   Thailand
Turkey   Ukraine   Vietnam

Oxford is a registered trade mark of Oxford University Press
in the UK and in certain other countries

Published in India
By Oxford University Press, New Delhi

© 2004 The World Bank, 1818 H Street, NW, Washington, DC 20433
First published in India 2004

ISBN 0 19 567332 8

Printed in India at Brijbasi Art Press Ltd, New Delhi 110 020
Published by Manzar Khan, Oxford University Press
YMCA Library Building, Jai Singh Road, New Delhi 110 001

■ Acknowledgements

This report was prepared by a multi-sectoral team led by Venita Kaul which included Meera Priyadarshi, (co-task leader), Peter Heywood, Suneeta Singh, Vandana Sipahimalani-Rao, Deepa Sankar and G.N.V. Ramana. The team would like to acknowledge the efforts put in by Kamal Gaur who provided academic support, S.A.A.Alvi who read through the final script meticulously and suggested improvements and Sudesh Ponnappa and Karthika Nair who provided excellent administrative support throughout, and more particularly in production of the final version of the report. The team appreciates the valuable feedback received from Michelle Riboud, Michael F. Carter and Shantayanan Devarajan, which helped in the improvement of the report. Grateful acknowledgement is also made of the contribution of Ward Heneveld for his continual guidance and support and of Mary Eming Young and Harold Alderman for their constructive contributions as peer reviewers.

The report draws on the following studies commissioned for this research – *A Conceptual Approach to Integrated Child Development* by New Concept Information Systems; *Empirical Analysis of the Conceptual Framework for Integrated Child Development* by Indicus Analytics; *Snakes and Ladders: Factors that Facilitate or Impede Successful Primary School Completion* by Vimala Ramachandran and her team; *Study of Existing Policies and Related Provisions and Schemes for Children* and *Public Spending on Child Development* by D.B. Gupta. The team would like to place on record its appreciation of the cooperation received from the researchers in terms of not only timely completion of the studies but also their receptivity to feedback.

The research benefited greatly from regular consultations with a Technical Committee of Indian professionals from Health, Education, Nutrition and Child Development sectors, particularly in developing the conceptual framework. The committee also included representatives from UNICEF and from the three concerned departments of Ministry of Human Resource Development, Government of India-Department of Elementary Education, Department of Health and Family Welfare and Department of Women and Child Development and some representatives from the states. The names of the members of the committee are annexed. The team would also like to express its gratitude especially to Dr. R.V.V. Ayyar and Mr. S.C. Tripathi, Secretaries of Department of Women and Child Development and Department of Elementary Education and Literacy and Dr. S. Anandalakshmy, Child Development Consultant for their participation and ideas shared in the seminar organized in this context in April 2003 and to Mr. Sumit Bose and Ms. Rekha Bhargava, Joint Secretaries for their contributions in all seminars held during the course of the research.

The report has been shared with Government of India, but does not necessarily bear approval for all its contents, especially where the Bank has stated its judgements, opinions and conclusions.

Abbreviations and Acronyms

ANM	Auxiliary Nurse Midwife		MDG	Millennium Development Goals
ARI	Acute Respiratory Infection		MIS	Monitoring and Information System
AWPB	Annual Work Plan and Budget		MMR	Maternal Mortality Rate
AS	Alternative Schools		MMS	Mid-day Meal Scheme
AWC	Anganwadi Centers		MHRD	Ministry of Human Resource Development
AWW	Anganwadi Worker		NCERT	National Council for Educational Research and Training
CDI	Child Development Index			
CSS	Centrally Sponsored Scheme		NFE	Non-Formal Education
CSSM	Child Survival and Safe Motherhood		NFHS	National Family Health Survey
DIET	District Institute of Education and Training		NGO	Non-Governmental Organization
			NIEPA	National Institute of Educational Planning and Administration
DOE	Department of Education			
DPEP	District Primary Education Program		NIPCCD	National Institute of Public Cooperation and Child Development
DPT	Diphtheria, Pertussis and Tetanus			
DWCD	Department of Women and Child Development		NSSO	National Sample Survey Organization
			OB	Operation Blackboard
ECCE	Early Childhood Care and Education		ORG	Operations Research Group
ECD	Early Childhood Development		ORT	Oral Rehydration Therapy
ECE	Early Childhood Education		PHC	Primary Health Center
EFA	Education for All		PMGY	Pradhan Mantri Gramodaya Yojana
EGS	Education Guarantee Scheme		PRI	Panchayati Raj Institution
EGS&AIE	Education Guarantee Scheme and Alternative Innovative Education		RCH	Reproductive and Child Health
			SERP	Society for Elimination of Rural Poverty
EMIS	Education Monitoring and Information Systems			
			SC	Scheduled Caste
GDP	Gross Domestic Product		SNP	Supplementary Nutrition Provision
ICD	Integrated Child Development		SSA	Sarva Shiksha Abhiyan
ICDS	Integrated Child Development Services		ST	Scheduled Tribe
			TN	Tamil Nadu
IEC	Information, Education, Communication		UEE	Universal Elementary Education
			UIP	Universal Immunization Program
IMR	Infant Mortality Rate		VEC	Village Education Committee
LBW	Low Birth Weight		VPD	Vaccine Preventable Disease
MCH	Maternal and Child Health			

▪ Contents

Tables

Boxes

Figures

⸬ Preface

What is the best investment we can make for India's future? "The development of children is the first priority on the country's development agenda, not because they are the most vulnerable, but because they are our supreme assets and also the future human resources of the country." In these words, India's Tenth Five Year Plan (2002-07) underlines the fact that the future of India lies in the future of Indian children – across income groups, geographical locations, gender and community. So, the best possible investment – the investment that promises the highest returns – is to ensure that every Indian child grows up in an environment conducive to her development. While India has, over the last few decades, made considerable progress in ensuring child survival and basic education, much remains to be done. When the major indicators for the Indian child's development – maternal mortality, birth weight, immunization, nutrition level and basic education – are compared with those of other developing countries, it is clear that the Indian child urgently needs better interventions. In the context of such a situation, the vision for the future has to be an India where all children have all the chances they need for optimal development. The emerging question is, despite significant investments and a conducive policy framework, why is the status of the Indian child still far from satisfactory? And, what then is the way forward to realize this vision?

It was in this context that a multi-sectoral workshop entitled "Reaching Out to the Child" was organized collaboratively by the Education and Health, Nutrition and Population teams of the World Bank on February 21 and 22, 2000 with the participation of Indian professionals from health, nutrition and education sectors; and senior representatives of the Departments of Health, Education, and Women and Child Development (WCD). The objective of the workshop was to initiate multi-sectoral discussions across the government and non-government sectors with the aim of establishing a constituency for the development of an integrated, comprehensive and convergent approach to child development. This involved, first of all, developing a shared vision of holistic child development, both across relevant sectors and throughout the process of development during the years of childhood. Next, it meant identifying critical outcome indicators and the corresponding inputs of optimal child development for each sub-stage of development. And third, it called for a review of the existing programs and services for children from an integrated and holistic perspective.

With this background of objectives, the workshop identified certain critical factors in the context of the Indian child's development:

1 A multi-sectoral approach to issues so as to capture the synergy of the different aspects of health, nutrition and education;

1 Adequate cognizance of the continuous and cumulative nature of child development through the different sub-stages, and within and across sectors; and

1 The essential input of proactively addressing not only the child, but also the child's immediate context, particularly the family and the community, to effectively reach the child.

On the basis of these factors, the possibility of using successful completion of primary schooling as an indicator of optimal child development, was proposed.

As an outcome of the workshop, a technical committee was constituted, consisting of experts in relevant fields and members of government, to meet periodically for consultations. With the guidance of this committee, two phases of activity emerged from the consultation. In the first phase, the New Concept Information Systems conducted a research review of literature on child development. This review, entitled "A Conceptual Approach to Integrated Child Development," examined both Indian and international research to determine the nature and dynamics of child development. On the basis of this research and its conclusions regarding the determinants, outcomes and indicators for each sub-stage of development from the prenatal stage to 11+ years, a conceptual framework was developed within the larger social environment context. This was done in consultation with the Technical Committee.

Using this conceptual framework as the guiding principle, four research studies were undertaken in the second phase: (i) The study by Indicus Analytics, *Empirical Analysis of the Conceptual Framework for Integrated Child Development,* applied multivariate and econometric analysis on sample based data from sources that have an all-India coverage – the National Family Health Surveys (NFHS-I and II); the Reproductive and Child Health Survey; and the National Sample Survey Organization The analysis was undertaken to assess the status of Indian children vis-a-vis the indicators and identify significant determinants at every sub-stage of development; (ii) A qualitative study of children from pre-natal to 11+ years in diverse poverty contexts was carried out by Vimala Ramchandran and her team from the Educational Resource Unit, New Delhi. This was done in three states – Andhra Pradesh, Karnataka, Uttar Pradesh. Entitled *Snakes and Ladders: Factors that Facilitate or Impede Successful Primary School Completion,* the study identified significant factors influencing the child's entry into school and successful completion of the primary education cycle. The study also elicited feedback on existing interventions for children; identified elements that affect child health, nutrition and education and their inter-

linkages; and examined implications for social policy; (iii) The research also included a report by Devendra B. Gupta, *Study of Existing Policies and Related Provisions and Schemes,* which analyzed policies and programs for the development needs of children from the prenatal sub-stage to 11+ years. The Report also reviewed, keeping in mind the priorities of the conceptual framework, the impact of current major provisions such as the Reproductive and Child Health Program, the Integrated Child Development Services Program, the Mid-day Meal Scheme and educational programs such as District Primary Education Program and *Sarva Shiksha Abhiyan*; and (iv) The Report *Public Spending on Child Development,* also by Devendra B.Gupta, updated and interpreted data on trends in government expenditure on child development, and discussed the way ahead for child-budgeting within the conceptual framework.

On completion of the five research studies, the main findings were presented to a multi-sectoral audience in a seminar in April 2003. As in the earlier workshop, the participants in this discussion included senior officials from the Departments of Elementary Education, Women and Child Development, Health and Family Welfare and Planning Commission as well as from some state governments and known professionals.

This report synthesizes the observations and conclusions from the five studies and the deliberations of the seminar, supplemented by review of other relevant documentation. The starting point of this report's conceptual framework is the premise that the child's development must be viewed along the prenatal to 11+ age continuum as a continuous and cumulative process. Investment and intervention have to take into account every sub-stage of the child's development process, from conception through the years of growth to enable the child at 11+ years to reach the basic milestone of successful completion of primary school. Moreover, intervention must account for the dynamic, interactive relationship among the sub-stages of development; among sectors such as health, nutrition and education; and among aspects such as maternal health, psychosocial development, and family and community environments. The continuous and cumulative nature of impact has also meant that the impact of not attaining appropriate developmental milestones, or health and nutritional outcomes, or learning capacities, will accompany the child to the next stage. In some cases, "cumulative" failure is the result of an inter-generational transfer of handicaps, and the accompanying downward spiral of poverty, ill health, malnutrition, and poor learning outcomes for children. For the purposes of the quantitative and qualitative data studies conducted for this report, the framework underlined the critical and reciprocal link between health and education, specifically in relation to children, whereby poor health and nutrition work as barriers to attendance and educational attainment/achievement. The family, the community, the state, service delivery mechanisms, and the presence of non-governmental organizations, all play important mediating roles and further fragment the experience at the grassroots.

Our research indicates that despite its potential, current social policy is unable to effectively capture and tap the positive synergy of the different sectoral interventions for a host of reasons. It is also unable to proactively harness the family and community in meeting its objectives of reaching the child, and creating a supportive environment for the child's development. On the whole, the research indicates that much needs to be done at policy as well as program levels. This report uses the data, the analysis and the conclusions of the studies to indicate the way ahead – whether it is for better nutrition, for better learning capacity or the achievement of physical, social and mental school readiness. It argues for more equipped, responsive and accountable schools; developmentally appropriate early childhood education, health-care and education, community participation and involvement; effective decentralized planning, targeting, spending, implementation and monitoring of programs, and the links among all these aspects.

Education, nutrition and development schemes need to be reviewed from this perspective. Given the size of the problem, and the complexity of issues involved, there is no alternative to a multi-sectoral and decentralized approach towards addressing the development and educational needs of Indian children, particularly in contexts of poverty and deprivation. Meeting their needs does not mean only more resources, but more care and attention at the levels of planning, program design and delivery, as well as monitoring and evaluation. Finally, children are active participants in the process of their development and education. Listening to children, and giving voice to their needs, is of the utmost importance.

■ Executive Summary

Introduction

This report is about Indian children and their development. It focuses on their physical, social, emotional, intellectual and educational development, all of which is not only a fundamental right of every child, but which also makes for a wholesome and capable individual, and thereby a competent society. The importance of ensuring optimal development of children, who are a nation's wealth, is based on the view that more than economic growth, it is the development of human capability in its population that makes a nation prosper. This implies that people's lives improve when they are free from illness, when they are well nourished and literate, and have self respect, work that matters and the freedom of choice. The process of developing these aspects of human capability begin in the earliest years of life, in early childhood.

But are the children in India really getting the childhood they deserve? This report is an attempt to address this concern. Based on the results of specially commissioned studies that have analyzed varied aspects of children's development in diverse poverty contexts, both in quantitative and qualitative terms, this report concludes that India has undoubtedly made considerable progress in the last two decades in promoting child survival and basic education. Along with a supportive policy framework, including the recent legislation to make elementary education a fundamental right, there have been in existence some major initiatives for children. More prominently, these are in the form of centrally sponsored schemes such as the Reproductive Child Health Scheme (RCH) in the Department of Health and Family Welfare, the Integrated Child Development Services (ICDS) in Department of Women and Child Development and several primary education schemes, including the District Primary Education Program (DPEP) and the government's flagship program, the *Sarva Shiksha Abhiyan* (SSA). As a result, noticeable progress has been made over the last fifty years, as seen in the rapid expansion of the ICDS and primary education service delivery network across the country.

Status of Children in India

In general, the report acknowledges that there has been progress on some child development parameters, such as the overall decline in childhood mortality, incidence of preventable diseases and increase in enrollments in primary schools. But, in comparison to other developing countries, progress in India has been slower, particularly on the Millennium Development Goals (MDGs). For instance, while Bangladesh and Nepal record a progress over the last decade (1990-2001) of 46 percent and 37 percent respectively in reduction in child mortality, India's progress is only 24 percent. A similar trend is seen on other indicators like gender equality and primary school completion. In terms of absolute levels also, for instance, while China's child mortality rate is 39 (in 2001) the corresponding rate for India is as high as 93, per thousand children. In terms of gender parity in elementary school enrolment, girls' enrolment as percentage of boys' enrolment is at 98 and 103 percent respectively in China and Bangladesh, while in India it is only 78 percent. India's primary school completion rate is only 76 percent as compared to China's 99 percent. The prospects of attaining the MDG targets – reducing the under-5 mortality rate by two-third, ensuring universal primary education and eliminating the gender disparity in primary education – by 2015 seem doubtful, given this current pace. As the review indicates, from conception to the stage of primary school completion, a large number of children continue to suffer from deficits which stem largely from poor maternal health, low birth weight, moderate to severe malnutrition, inadequate psycho-social stimulation and disability. All of these, in isolation and cumulatively, can adversely affect the probability of children developing optimally, entering and attending school regularly and completing the primary cycle of education. These factors are further compounded by other environmental and social factors such as gender and caste, inadequate family and community support and poor quality of service delivery in all sectors including health care, water and sanitation, preschool and primary schooling.

However, there are wide variations across the states. These variations are evident in the inter-state comparisons made on the Child Development Index (CDI) computed specially for this research, using some important indicators related to survival and education outcomes. While Bihar is on one end of the spectrum with a CDI of 49 on a 100 scale, Himachal Pradesh and Kerala are at the other end with indices at 91 and 92 respectively. The analysis also reveals that states that perform poorly on one indicator repeat the poor performance on most related indicators, reflecting a cumulative and concentrated pattern of disadvantage, which is indicative of a definite inter-dependence of outcomes. These poorer states include Bihar, Rajasthan, Uttar Pradesh, West Bengal and Assam. Interestingly, even across these poorer performing states there is a wide range. The fact that their status continues to be low despite the centrally sponsored schemes supplementing their own state level efforts over the last two to three decades, indicates that the success of these schemes has been, by and large, not commensurate with the investments made.

Emerging Issues

What could be the reasons for this limited impact of existing provisions for children? Some factors identified in the report include (a) a fragmented, sectoral approach in implementing the schemes, which does not capture the synergies across sectors, (b) over-centralized and standardized program designs which do not address contextual diversities, (c) inadequate finances and inefficient implementation, (d) inadequate monitoring capacity and (e) low accountability and issues of service delivery.

Interdependence of outcomes requires a holistic approach

Why is the sectoral/compartmentalized approach an issue? Historically, the experience may have been that this specialized approach was advantageous for ensuring more focused attention. In the area of child development, however, the sectoral approach becomes an issue since it runs counter to the globally accepted evidence regarding how children develop. More specifically, it disregards the significant inter-dependence of health, nutrition and educational outcomes, across the sub stages of a child's development which calls for integrated implementation of sectoral programs, and not a sector-specific approach. This holistic approach is based on an understanding of the interdependence of outcomes at two levels – vertical and lateral; (a) vertically, it is seen in terms of the continuous and cumulative nature of the process of a child's development, so that every preceding sub-stage tends to set the readiness level for the next sub-stage and (b) laterally, it is in terms of the synergistic relationship evident across the human development aspects or sub-sectors, i.e. health, nutrition and education.

The vertical linkages are essentially linear and require the entire childhood continuum to be addressed in totality, while planning for children. Their importance rests on the empirical evidence that the first six years of childhood are critical for brain development and development of several important social, cognitive and linguistic skills that are important for success in later life. Research in neurosciences indicates that by age three, 85 percent of the child's core brain structure is already formed and any deficits resulting from a deficient environment in these early years may be very difficult to reverse later. Given the crucial importance of the early years and the fact that child development is a cumulative process, it becomes imperative to ensure that every child crosses each sub stage of the development continuum

successfully, before progressing to the next stage. If a child falters in one or more milestones, the child carries in either latent or cumulative terms, the burden of failure to the next stage. International evidence, reviewed in the report, confirms in this context the positive impact of ECD interventions in compensating for home deficits and improving children's life chances. The impact is proven in both long and short term perspectives. The long term impact is seen in terms of higher levels of psychosocial competence and adjustment in both family and professional contexts that is demonstrated by adults who have had ECD experience, as compared to those who have not. The shorter term impact is evident on primary education outcomes. Research in India and elsewhere, particularly affirms a significant impact of ECD interventions on the MDG goal of primary enrolment, attendance, completion and learning achievement of children and also on facilitating participation of girls in primary schooling. ECD is thus also seen to reduce investment costs of subsequent interventions at the primary stage by reducing drop outs and repetition, improving efficiency and contributing significantly to the goals of education for all. However, while the impact is proven, the concern is that the present coverage of children utilizing any kind of early childhood development interventions in India is still only around 15 percent, across the country, despite the expansion of ICDS and private sector provisions.

Research reviewed across the globe also confirms the lateral 'inter dependence' of health, nutrition and education outcomes. There is evidence to indicate the significant influence of malnutrition in children on their ability to attend to and comprehend instruction, on their activity level, concentration and overall ability to learn. Field experience in India, substantiated by research, also indicates impact of short term illnesses like malaria and diarrhea on regularity of children's attendance in schools, which in turn influences the learning outcomes. These also suggest obvious linkages with outcomes in other sectors such as for example, availability of water and proper sanitation, the absence of which leads to frequent diarrhea, malaria and other epidemics.

Given the interdependence of outcomes, it follows logically that the factors in implementation are also mutually dependent, since these must converge on a common target group or beneficiaries in a timely manner to optimize their synergistic impact. For example, unless the water and sanitation facilities are ensured, health outcomes will be affected, which in turn will influence regular participation of children in primary schooling. Deriving from such interrelationships, investments in primary education will have limited impact unless corresponding interventions are also ensured for the same set of beneficiaries in health and nutrition and other related sectors by way of, for example, an effective mid day meal program and an effective school health program. Similarly, the issue of child labor will be better addressed through supplementing primary education facilities with an effective income generation program for the family. Unless these are adequately addressed in a comprehensive way, primary education outcomes, through purely education sector interventions, cannot be guaranteed.

Contextual diversities demand decentralized planning

Another concern with most centrally sponsored schemes for children is that their program design is, in most cases, very centralized and standardized, with total disregard of contextual diversities, particularly in a large country like India. The scheme in such cases tends to get implemented in a supply driven mode with little ownership from the beneficiaries. This research has clearly indicated that there are not only wide inter state variations, but also within states, districts and sub district

levels there can be differences in contexts and priorities for children's development. A recent study showed how nutrition interventions from the government were going to a community which had no incidence of malnutrition in children, due to adequate provisions in the home backyards! The priority in this community was an efficient PHC and quality pre-school and primary education, which were not getting addressed! Given the scarcity of resources, ensuring the right interface between community demand and government driven supply becomes necessary, for which program designs are required that would allow for local specificity and prioritization. This can be possible only through participatory approaches to planning and implementation that involve the actual beneficiaries.

Services for children are there, but where is the accountability?

Accountability of service providers to the poor communities is another significant issue related to service delivery, which needs to be addressed through more active stakeholder participation. Children of the poor have affordable access only to lower quality provisions, often dysfunctional and inefficient because of corruption and low accountability, whether it is the health provision or *anganwadi* services or primary schooling. And they also have no voice that can make a difference As the 2004 World Development Report analyses, services are failing the poor in four ways. Firstly, while government spending on education and health may increase over years (even though they remain well below international comparisons), spending on actual quality of services on the ground necessary to improve the status of the children of the poor is still minimal. Secondly, even when public spending is reallocated towards the poor, it often does not reach the frontline provider. Thirdly, service providers are often mired in a system where the incentives for effective service delivery are weak, wages may not be paid, corruption is rife and political patronage is a way of life. This together with inadequate mechanisms for accountability in the system leads to a placid acceptance and perpetuation of inefficiency. The fourth way services fail the poor is due to lack of demand or differences in perceptions with the community. These could be due to social or economic factors or also often due to lack of information, as seen in the case of preference for home over institutional deliveries due to economic reasons, or for private schools due to the attraction of learning English which results in reducing pressure on the public system to improve. An important factor is the lack of ownership of the service offered, among the community, which deters the user groups from identifying with the program, and accepting their own role in taking responsibility and/or ensuring accountability.

Is financing addressing children's needs holistically?

Inadequate financing and inefficient spending also influence the impact of programs on ground for fostering children's development. An analysis carried out for this research indicates that the state governments do spend, on an average, around 10 percent of their total budget on children, but this camouflages a wide range. Also, a substantial component of this spending is on salaries, leaving little scope for investment in areas that would improve targeting and service delivery. The central government support, through its centrally sponsored schemes, can add value, but the analysis indicates that central spending on children is less than 2 percent of the overall central government's budget. The central and state governments' spending together on children's development adds up to only 2.65 percent of the GDP. The concern is that in a country of 20 million children below 11 years, this amounts to a paltry sum of about US $ 1.8 per child per month!

With respect to budgeting for children, *three* specific imbalances stand out. *First*, in terms of inter-sectoral comparisons, the priority in both central and state government spending has been biased towards primary education, with its share being as high as 56 percent of the total spending on children. Consequently, improvements in CDI over the years are attributable largely to improved enrollments in primary education and much less to progress on the nutrition and health indicators. A *second* imbalance is with regard to relative spending on children below 6 years and that for the 6+ years. Despite the critical importance of the first six years of life which set the foundation for life long development, actual spending per child on children below 6 years is almost one-eighth of that on children in the 6-14 age group, across all states. This indicates a gross neglect of the foundation years of childhood. A *third* imbalance is seen in the resources available to and being spent by the weaker states, as compared to those more advanced. States with the poorest indicators may need more but actually get less and also spend less per child on major programs for children. This imbalance is also evident in the wide gap observed between the states' needs estimated on per child basis by the Planning Commission and the actual departmental allocations, which are possibly influenced by the limited absorptive and implementation capacity of the states. This suggests the *perpetuation of a vicious cycle* of low resources and slow development, which adversely affects the pace of development in the weaker states. It, thus, makes a strong case in all projects for investing concurrently on institutional reforms, along with the funding, to ensure both adequacy of resources and their efficient use.

Monitoring progress – lack of a tangible indicator

A constraint in effectively promoting child development through public services is the difficulty in monitoring progress and impact, particularly in the absence of tangible and monitorable indicators. This difficulty is especially with regard to the more qualitative but critical dimensions of integrated child development. In this context, this research identifies 'successful completion of primary education', which is globally considered a significant milestone at the end of the childhood stage, as a concrete proxy indicator of overall optimal child development. The rationale is that, given the cumulative process of child development and the inter dependence of outcomes, it can be deduced that the probability of successful primary school completion will be determined by the status of a child's health, nutrition and educational outcomes, along all sub stages of the continuum. Successful primary school completion therefore indicates a status of overall satisfactory development of the child. Identification of this indicator is justified on empirical grounds also, which indicate that not only are economic returns highest for primary education but primary education, particularly for women, leads to better family health, lower fertility, and a better quality of life for the child and the family. An important implication of this is that the holistic 'child development' approach should not be limited to the early childhood stage only, as is conventionally believed, but should get extended to the primary stage as well. *Successful completion of primary education is defined here not in the narrow sense as mere completion of the five primary grades and acquisition of literacy and numeracy, but in addition, demonstration of attributes like active learning capacity, positive self esteem, good health/nutritional status and good habits and values in children.*

The Way Forward

The Tenth Five-Year Plan has set targets for child development and education for the country that are even more ambitious than the Millennium Development Goals. The need of the hour is to therefore determine what the way forward should be, which will help realize these goals on the fast track to which GOI is committed. A major objective would be to universalize the coverage of ECD provisions such as Reproductive Child Health (RCH) and Integrated Child Development (ICDS) (interventions include maternal health, safe delivery, care of newborn, nutrition security including breastfeeding and complementary and responsive feeding, caregiver-child interaction, management of childhood illnesses, childcare practices, pre-school care and education, family and community support, environmental hygiene, safe water and sanitation, cultural attitudes and contexts), which at present cover only 15 percent of the child population. Equally important would be the objective of ensuring quality of service delivery to attain the identified developmental outcomes for children, at all sub stages of child development. Does the fast track require up-scaling and expansion of existing modes of provision for children or does it require a change in track? The analysis shows that there has to be a shift, both in the policy paradigm guiding the interventions for the Indian child and in programming, if the desired outcomes are to be realized. The recommendations that follow suggest a possible direction.

Moving towards an outcome-focused and child-centered approach to planning for children

If getting all children to successfully complete primary education is the goal, what are the expected outcomes along the way from birth onwards that would enhance the probability, and what are their indicators and determinants? This would be crucial information required for all holistic planning and programming for children. Based on a comprehensive review of Indian and international researches, this report presents an *Integrated Conceptual Framework* (Figure1) which identifies these expected outcomes, determinants and indicators along the child development trajectory. *This framework can be a useful source of reference for policy makers and program implementers for planning and providing for children in a comprehensive*

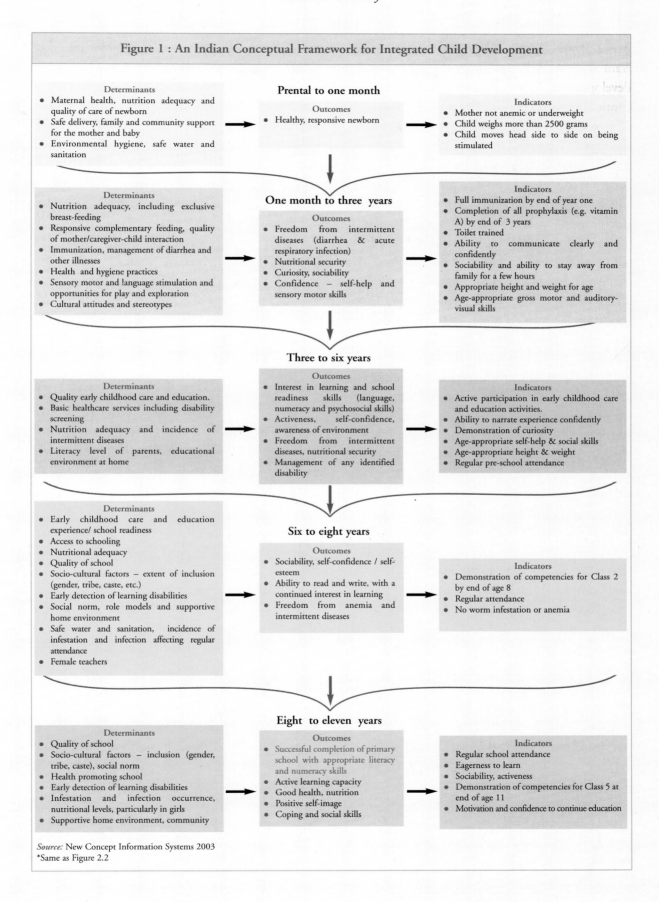

Figure 1 : An Indian Conceptual Framework for Integrated Child Development

Prental to one month

Determinants
- Maternal health, nutrition adequacy and quality of care of newborn
- Safe delivery, family and community support for the mother and baby
- Environmental hygiene, safe water and sanitation

Outcomes
- Healthy, responsive newborn

Indicators
- Mother not anemic or underweight
- Child weighs more than 2500 grams
- Child moves head side to side on being stimulated

One month to three years

Determinants
- Nutrition adequacy, including exclusive breast-feeding
- Responsive complementary feeding, quality of mother/caregiver-child interaction
- Immunization, management of diarrhea and other illnesses
- Health and hygiene practices
- Sensory motor and language stimulation and opportunities for play and exploration
- Cultural attitudes and stereotypes

Outcomes
- Freedom from intermittent diseases (diarrhea & acute respiratory infection)
- Nutritional security
- Curiosity, sociability
- Confidence – self-help and sensory motor skills

Indicators
- Full immunization by end of year one
- Completion of all prophylaxis (e.g. vitamin A) by end of 3 years
- Toilet trained
- Ability to communicate clearly and confidently
- Sociability and ability to stay away from family for a few hours
- Appropriate height and weight for age
- Age-appropriate gross motor and auditory-visual skills

Three to six years

Determinants
- Quality early childhood care and education.
- Basic healthcare services including disability screening
- Nutrition adequacy and incidence of intermittent diseases
- Literacy level of parents, educational environment at home

Outcomes
- Interest in learning and school readiness skills (language, numeracy and psychosocial skills)
- Activeness, self-confidence, awareness of environment
- Freedom from intermittent diseases, nutritional security
- Management of any identified disability

Indicators
- Active participation in early childhood care and education activities.
- Ability to narrate experience confidently
- Demonstration of curiosity
- Age-appropriate self-help & social skills
- Age-appropriate height & weight
- Regular pre-school attendance

Six to eight years

Determinants
- Early childhood care and education experience/ school readiness
- Access to schooling
- Nutritional adequacy
- Quality of school
- Socio-cultural factors – extent of inclusion (gender, tribe, caste, etc.)
- Early detection of learning disabilities
- Social norm, role models and supportive home environment
- Safe water and sanitation, incidence of infestation and infection affecting regular attendance
- Female teachers

Outcomes
- Sociability, self-confidence / self-esteem
- Ability to read and write, with a continued interest in learning
- Freedom from anemia and intermittent diseases

Indicators
- Demonstration of competencies for Class 2 by end of age 8
- Regular attendance
- No worm infestation or anemia

Eight to eleven years

Determinants
- Quality of school
- Socio-cultural factors – inclusion (gender, tribe, caste), social norm
- Health promoting school
- Early detection of learning disabilities
- Infestation and infection occurrence, nutritional levels, particularly in girls
- Supportive home environment, community

Outcomes
- Successful completion of primary school with appropriate literacy and numeracy skills
- Active learning capacity
- Good health, nutrition
- Positive self-image
- Coping and social skills

Indicators
- Regular school attendance
- Eagerness to learn
- Sociability, activeness
- Demonstration of competencies for Class 5 at end of age 11
- Motivation and confidence to continue education

Source: New Concept Information Systems 2003
*Same as Figure 2.2

manner, keeping the focus on outcomes. This framework argues for addressing the overall developmental needs of children along the entire continuum, from pre natal stage all the way up-to 11+ years by when children are expected to successfully complete primary education. It also indicates the developmental priorities for each sub stage of childhood, which if taken care of in a timely manner will reduce costs of subsequent interventions and optimize impact, leading to attainment of the MDGs. For example, the priority for the 0-3 year period is nutritional security since this is the critical period for brain development. It is also the stage when the child is most vulnerable to growth faltering. If this is addressed in a timely way, it will arrest the problem of malnutrition in children before it becomes endemic and difficult to reverse later. It will also help children realize their full brain potential. The framework also emphasizes the interdependent and synergistic nature of health, nutrition and educational outcomes and the need for related interventions in the context of not only the child but also the child's immediate and extended environment.

Moving from a sectoral towards a multi-sectoral approach

The overall message of the research is that children's developmental and educational needs are very closely interlinked and should therefore be approached in a coherent multi-sectoral manner. However, this does not imply addressing all needs for all sub stages through a single integrated program. For example, the ICDS is required to cover, in all, six services for children between 0-6 years. And all these are to be delivered through one lone worker and her helper at the end point of service delivery. After almost thirty years of program implementation of ICDS, its gains are being questioned. The program has neither been able to significantly reduce malnutrition in children nor ensure quality pre school education! The implication of this recommendation is therefore that, since process of implementation is interdependent,

the *planning and monitoring of children's provisions should be done for all children in the 0-11+ age range judiciously and jointly across related sectors, in a coordinated and complementary manner.* The important message is – plan for the WHOLE CHILD and not for education, health and nutrition separately.

This holistic planning could, at all levels, be guided by the following questions:

- What are the development and educational outcomes desirable for children at each sub-stage, taking into account the community's own priorities, so that the probability of successful completion of basic schooling is enhanced? (As in Framework)

- What are the essential conditions and interventions necessary to realize the expected outcomes?

- Which scheme or sector has the comparative advantage of delivering these conditions?

- How can the status of these outcomes be assessed/ monitored regularly?

This may have implications for reviewing current administrative arrangements and distribution of responsibilities. A case in point is the provision for Early Childhood Education for 3 to 6 year olds which is presently the mandate of the Department of Women and Child Development, and routed for delivery mainly through the ICDS. Is the design of ICDS best suited for this intervention, given its habitation based structure and six services? Evaluation studies under DPEP have shown that the habitation-based ICDS center is more conducive to meet the needs of the children under 3 years of age and pregnant women. In comparison, the school-based early childhood education model is relatively better placed to deliver early childhood education to 3-6 year olds, since it promotes early bonding with school, ensures greater curricular continuity, and frees older girls from sibling care to participate in schooling. There is, therefore, a need to examine whether the Department of Women and Child Development should be responsible for pregnant and lactating women and for crèches and play-centers for children under 3 years, while the Department of Education takes on early childhood education for the 3-6 year-olds, as part of its elementary school system.

Moving from a supply driven to a demand driven, community based approach

Reaching outcomes would require moving from a schematic supply-driven approach, which typically adopts a standardized model across the country with discrete components and stringent norms, to a more bottom up approach which would reflect community needs and priorities. *Given the wide diversity and the need to ensure the right inter-face between the community driven demand at the local levels and the government driven supply, involving the community, that is the actual beneficiaries, in participatory planning for children becomes a priority.* This would essentially require a self-assessment of the community needs and demands, acknowledged and articulated by itself, which should be a first step towards establishing subsequent ownership of the planned interventions. However, while participatory planning has been adopted in programs in Water and Sanitation and Education sectors, the learning from both sectors has been that (a) it is important to ensure upfront who is the 'community' that is being involved – to what extent do the 'community members' who are involved in the planning, actually represent the interests and needs of the larger community, particularly the poorest of the poor and (b) the process of participatory planning and community mobilization requires considerable amount of training initially alongwith hand holding of the community members by NGOs or program staff, for some time, before it really gets into motion.

The role of a facilitator or facilitating agency is therefore important.

Using information in a planned way to educate, communicate and involve the community: Educating the community about children's developmental needs and the role the community can play in meeting these, is very important not only from the point of view of influencing the quality of their own interactions with their children but also to help them identify and articulate their priorities with regard to their children better. This need is evident, for example, in the misplaced preference parents often show in buying strong medicines off the shelf for the children or in choosing an academic kind of ECD program, which is a downward extension of primary education and inappropriate for children, due to lack of information regarding the consequences. Also, *educating the community and making information transparent can serve an even more important purpose of opening up alternative service delivery mechanisms and encouraging greater accountability of providers to poorer communities, both through demand side factors and also through empowering the poor, as citizens, to bring pressure on the politicians and bureaucracy to improve services for children.* A vital component of this education should be to help the community identify the outcomes that they must ensure in their children and towards which they should work.

In this context more resources and better planning are needed for the Information, Education and Communication (IEC) component of programs. The lesson learnt from previous projects is that the IEC component should be built into all social projects but the messages should be formulated using a client-oriented approach that moves away from western models to a more contextually relevant content and approach. Use of both folk and electronic media can be very powerful, as seen in the polio campaigns, particularly when celebrities have been brought in to advocate the message. Another lesson learnt from revisiting earlier nutrition education and preventive health programs is the need to front-load this component in any program, in terms of the time frame, so as to provide adequate time for attitudinal change. Frontloading would also allow for better informed utilization of the program interventions and more effective monitoring by the community. In this context, direct community contact through campaigns like the UNICEF's *Meena* campaign, have been particularly effective, especially if compared to the doubtful impact of "text based messages" seen all over, which are mis-directed at illiterate targets.

Moving from centralized and standardized program designs towards decentralized planning – preparing village/ward plans for children

Given the wide diversities in India, a standardized model, as adopted in many centrally sponsored schemes, cannot be expected to effectively reach every child in the country, particularly the ones that need it the most. The need therefore is for a more contextualized and decentralized program design. The current shift in many states towards the *Panchayat Raj* or local self-government, especially in the social sector, is likely to allow greater space for this to become possible. Experience in DPEP and the ongoing SSA programs in decentralized district based planning, which in turn rests on village based educational plans, has been quite positive. This has also involved devolution of administrative control to the panchayat /village level, as seen for example in the delegation of powers to local authorities to appoint and pay teachers, construct and maintain schools, monitor teacher attendance according to their local requirements and oversee their functioning. The limitation comes in however, when the norms by which they can do this are still centralized and fixed. This may, to some extent, limit more creative and local alternatives to emerge

in terms of, for example, choice of alternative providers and other untried interventions.

Drawing on the more innovative experiences of these schemes and the recent designing of the RCH scheme on a similar pattern, this report *recommends extending the idea further of Village Education/Health Plans which are still limited to sectoral outcomes, into preparation of more comprehensive, multi-sectoral Village/ Ward Plans for Children. The suggestion is to move beyond the current practice of planning in a compartmentalized way for health, education, nutrition separately, as is being currently done under different sectoral schemes to plan for the child as a whole.* This compartmentalized approach is known to often lead to duplication and wastage of inputs and resources. These Village/Ward Plans, based on joint planning, would holistically cover children from pre natal to 11+ years in the focused area, and for each sub stage take into account the specific developmental priorities related to health, nutrition, education, safety, sanitation etc. This would also take into account special needs of the marginalized groups, such as girls, children with disabilities, working children, street children and SC/ST children. The intention should be to converge related provisions for children in a complementary manner towards promoting the all round development of every child in the area. These plans could be aggregated as district plans and these could set a common agenda for the donors and stakeholders interested in working for children in a given community, which could then be addressed through sharing of costs and responsibilities and a common framework of monitoring.

The process of development of this Village/ Ward Plan for Children is envisaged through active and informed participation of the community/beneficiaries, with representation from all habitations within the identified area. Since the

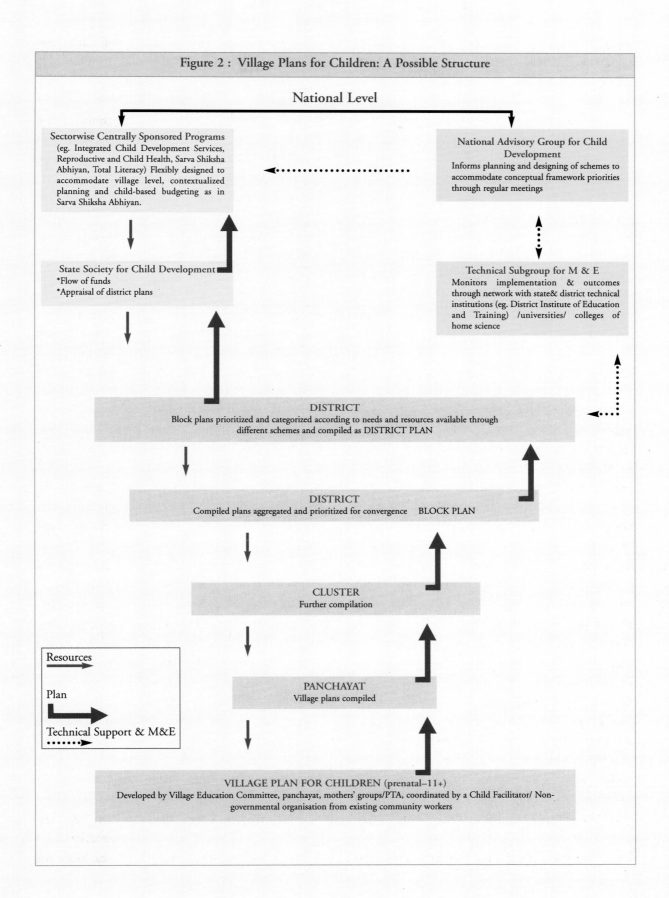

Figure 2 : Village Plans for Children: A Possible Structure

National Level

Sectorwise Centrally Sponsored Programs (eg. Integrated Child Development Services, Reproductive and Child Health, Sarva Shiksha Abhiyan, Total Literacy) Flexibly designed to accommodate village level, contextualized planning and child-based budgeting as in Sarva Shiksha Abhiyan.

National Advisory Group for Child Development
Informs planning and designing of schemes to accommodate conceptual framework priorities through regular meetings

State Society for Child Development
*Flow of funds
*Appraisal of district plans

Technical Subgroup for M & E
Monitors implementation & outcomes through network with state& district technical institutions (eg. District Institute of Education and Training) /universities/ colleges of home science

DISTRICT
Block plans prioritized and categorized according to needs and resources available through different schemes and compiled as DISTRICT PLAN

DISTRICT
Compiled plans aggregated and prioritized for convergence   BLOCK PLAN

CLUSTER
Further compilation

PANCHAYAT
Village plans compiled

VILLAGE PLAN FOR CHILDREN (prenatal–11+)
Developed by Village Education Committee, panchayat, mothers' groups/PTA, coordinated by a Child Facilitator/ Non-governmental organisation from existing community workers

Resources

Plan

Technical Support & M&E

participatory process would need considerable hand holding and training in the initial years before the confidence and capability is developed, it would be necessary to locate a nodal person/organization from among existing community based functionaries, (for example the head teachers, multi purpose *panchayat* workers, literacy animators /motivators, active *anganwadi* workers or a team of these or a local non-government organization with a good track record) who could be trained as community-based Child Facilitators to mobilize the community and facilitate the process of preparing village/ward plans. This proposal could be piloted initially under existing schemes through convergence, before up-scaling.

For this decentralized approach to be effective, an essential condition would be the devolution of much greater autonomy and freedom of choice at the existing decentralized, community levels. The ultimate vision guiding this concept of community ownership is to have block funds made available to local communities which would enable them to choose and 'buy' services from the line bureaucracies, or NGOs or the private sector locally to address their plans for their children. The accountability would be in terms of their responsibility for the identified and agreed outcomes. However, this change over to total autonomy will have to be gradual, given the current centralized arrangements and schemes with the line ministries and the resistance to change. For effecting this transition, some measures could be considered. One possibility for bringing in a natural convergence and accountability in the current system could be to issue 'child development progress cards' for every child from 0-11+ years, by the local *Panchayat* or School Management Committee. This card could track children's progress across some prioritized cross-sectoral indicators agreed with the community, such as birth weight, immunization, nutritional level, pre-school participation etc. leading up to

school completion. These cards could then be collated to report on the Village/Ward child development status and publicized and/or further aggregated into the CDI. Another possible implementation modality for accelerating this transition towards convergent planning, based on the current experiences with the Education and RCH schemes, is displayed in Figure 2, and described in greater detail in the report.

Improving targeting and monitoring

Given clusters of poor children in specific regions, states and districts that continue to remain untouched by any of the current interventions, *better targeting of services and provisions is a priority.* Through the proposed process of decentralized village/ward based planning, the possibility of reaching every child across the country becomes more real. Along with decentralized planning, at a macro level, systems of monitoring and evaluation also need to be made more robust in terms of both data availability, reliability, and capacity at all levels to use data meaningfully. Several databases are available at present in India including the Census of India 2001 data and computerized household census data under SSA which is documented in Village Education Registers and updated annually. Where available, this data will facilitate the identification of vulnerable groups, child labor, girls, tribals, poor and disabled children and their special needs. If reliable, these data sets will also enable a system of child tracking and child-specific interventions as a part of the proposed Village/Ward Plan for children. *The research recommends that particular attention be given to issues of data use and data quality, for which appropriate systems need to be in place. There should also be an emphasis on systematic trialing and impact evaluation of interventions before up-scaling.* To be effective this would need attitudinal change at all levels to start looking at data not merely as a reporting activity, but as a tool for diagnosis and planning and also for bringing in more transparency into decision making. This would require efforts towards 'demystification of data' at decentralized levels, since ensuring capacity in effective use of data at community levels will be particularly important.

Improving service delivery

Experience shows that services for children, whether through the *Anganwadi* (ECD Centre) or the primary school, get utilized and owned by the community only to the extent that the service delivered is perceived to be of value by the community. On the other hand, quality on such a large scale can only be assured through greater community involvement, oversight and ownership. *This vicious cycle of poor quality leading to less community involvement, needs to be broken through by addressing quality of service delivery* in terms of (a) understanding and influencing the nature of community demand and identifying and ensuring basic conditions for quality – be it in a school, or *anganwadi* including physical facilities, effective local leadership, rationalization of roles and responsibilities for example of an *anganwadi* worker, the ANM and school teachers; (b) setting conditions for meeting the community's right to information and transparency through social audit; for example putting up information regarding the devolved funds to school committees on the school notice board, as in DPEP or publishing education grants to school districts in Ugandan newspapers and developing community ownership of the service offered; (c) educating the community, particularly the poor, to empower them as citizens to bring pressure on the administrators and politicians to improve services for children for example, the Bangalore Citizen report cards or the use of media to regularly publish stories of success and failures in service delivery in Andhra Pradesh; (d) By bringing in greater focus on outcomes through, for instance, maintaining and publicizing aggregated information from the child

development report cards- for *panchayats* to make them more accountable; and (e) introducing some incentive mechanisms, monitory or related to the career ladder, to reward performance and motivate the frontline workers.

Making private sector more accountable and forging new partnerships

Improving quality of service delivery also requires taking on the issue of forging other new institutional arrangements and partnerships. Though the public sector obviously bears the central responsibility of catering to the Indian child's needs, it needs additional partners – new and innovative relationship with and among the business community, the private sector, non governmental organizations (NGOs), institutions and professional bodies. A good example could be the initiative in Nepal to address the challenge of universalizing access to early childhood education through tripartite partnerships between funding agencies, NGOs and Village development committees, using the concept of matching funds by community for sustainability and following common guidelines.

Whether it is *the reality of "health" being bought across the counter, or private schools being sought because of a perception of better quality, the reality of the private sector presence needs to be now officially acknowledged. This is necessary so that there can be adequate and appropriate regulation, whether through direct government intervention (which has its attendant problems) or more effectively through making the community more vigilant and informed as consumers through an effective IEC initiative.* Alongside the regulation, possibilities of using the private sector more to deliver services can also be considered for example by giving poor families vouchers (as *Progressa/ Opportunidades* in Mexico does) or quotas in private schools as stipulated by the Supreme Court in India or introducing incentives for quality improvement such as the Learning Guarantee Scheme being implemented by the WIPRO Foundation in Karnataka.

Investing in the very young child – a priority

There is adequate empirical evidence of the significant and positive impact of early childhood development interventions on subsequent enrollment, attendance and retention at the primary stage. Investment in the early years is therefore known to make subsequent investments more cost effective. In the Brazilian PROAPE project, for example, the total costs of schooling, including the early learning program itself, for pupils up-to grade 2 was 11 percent lower for those who participated in the early childhood development program, as compared to those who did not. Yet, trends analyzed across India indicate that the spending on children below 6 years is approximately 8 times less than that on children above 6 years. Given the fact that brain development is fastest in the first few years of life, which makes the early childhood period critical for life-long learning, this disparity in investment is clearly a misplaced priority. *This research therefore makes an emphatic recommendation for addressing this investment gap by proportionately increasing spending on the early childhood years, alongside for primary education, nutrition and health of 6-14 year olds, to ensure all children in the country get the opportunity to develop optimally.*

Targeting public financing for poor children

The issue of inadequacy of financial provision for children has already been discussed, particularly in the context of the less progressive states. In addition, it was observed that in those states in which the need was greater, the resource gap in terms of actual allocations was also wider. A possible intervening factor could be the weak absorptive capacity of the states. *This suggests a vicious cycle of low resources, weak capacity and poor development, typical of many northern states in India, which needs to be urgently broken.* Given the limited resources available with the government and its track record of service delivery, the question arises – to what extent and where should government at the Federal and provincial levels, put to use its limited resources, so that the returns are significant. The World Development Report (2004) provides a framework for thinking through this question. Inferring from this framework, there is no ambiguity in that the government will have to be the dominant provider for children's development and education due to the pro-poor focus, heterogeneous nature of interventions and complexity of monitoring of provisions related to children. *However, considerations of equity and efficiency coupled with the constraints of limited resources and the need for maximizing welfare impact, call for a rational targeting of public resources for the poorest of the poor;* alongside this, efforts are required to mobilize/encourage private investment through a policy based on combination of incentives and regulation, so as to enable wider access. Possibilities of cost sharing and pooling of resources by multiple stakeholders, in support of a common framework, could also be a way forward to ensure wider coverage and better quality. In addition to enhanced funding through multiple sources, the study also recommends *the need for governance and administrative reforms and greater focus in all projects on strengthening institutional capacity, which would enable the money allocated to be spent with greater accountability, greater focus on outcomes, and most of all, with less risk of perpetuating inequities.*

Introduction
DEVELOPMENT
FOR A LIFETIME

▬ Introduction
Development for a Lifetime

Poor Children's Lives: Snakes and Ladders

Six-year-old Munni, from Nizamabad District in Andhra Pradesh, is a special child. She was born with a congenital problem and multiple disabilities. Her father studied up to Class 10 but has no regular employment, so he works as a daily wage laborer. Munni's mother and eldest sister (who dropped out of school) sell steel vessels. Munni herself is enrolled in the local anganwadi center (ECD center), but her parents never send her there. "What if the other children tease her? Or the teacher and helper don't take care of her"? they ask. Instead, Munni's second sister Surya, all of ten years old, skips school to look after Munni as well as the household. Surya is a loving sister, and fusses over Munni, playing with her and responding to her crying instantly.

But obviously the rest is beyond little Surya's abilities. Munni is not bathed or cleaned often; her nails are overgrown and her hair is matted. Her legs are covered with scabies. She scratches the wounds, and some of them are filled with pus, attracting flies.

Faraway in Uttar Pradesh, eleven-year-old Punnu, a son of the poorest family in his village, is supposed to be in Class IV. But he is not in school often. His new teacher is too fond of the cane, and Punnu can barely read and write. And anyway, he is not likely to study beyond primary school. So he spends most of his time playing cards with other village boys, grazing the cattle his family is taking care of, or swimming in the river, perhaps catching a fish for the family meal on a lucky day.[1]

The early years of a child's life last a lifetime …

---

[1] Ramachandran et al 2003.

Development has to be a cumulative and continuous process, starting at conception, and following the child's lifecycle.

Shifting the Focus to People

These are two equally real faces of poverty. For children like Munni and Punnu who suffer from malnutrition, poor health, a lack of learning opportunities and limited choices, development — *changing their experiences so they have a way out of poverty into better lives* – cannot be something abstract. Or something seen only in terms of "income growth". Markets and incomes are important, but only to the extent that they help people live healthier and more fulfilling lives. If Munni's and Punnu's lives are to grow and change, the focus must be on them and their families as people. And it is when these people are "more able to achieve what makes their lives valuable" that development occurs.[2] People's lives improve when they are free from illness, when they are well nourished and literate, have self-respect, have work that matters, and a sense of choice. This shift — from seeing economic growth as an end in itself to promoting the process of "expanding the real freedoms that people enjoy" — is at the heart of the more comprehensive human capability approach.

When do we begin Developing Human Capability?

To develop the capability of Munni and Punnu, and their numerous sisters and brothers across India, a one-time input – a specific program or a school, for example – is simply not enough. If the human capability of real people is to be developed,

it has to be done through a process of cumulative and continuous development following their lifecycle. Such a process begins with a solid foundation in the childhood years – from the point of conception, through infancy, and the pre-school and then on to the school stage.

Why focus on the early years? The first six years of a child's life, and more particularly the first three years, are critical for lifelong development. Environmental conditions, such as nutrition security, health and psychological stimulation, influence the way a child's neural pathways grow and the brain's circuitry wired. By the age of three, a child's brain is twice as active as that of an adult.[3] This head-start continues for the first decade making it all the more important for the child to use her/his brain at the right time – or lose out on its potential. If a child falters in one or more of the development milestones – health and nutrition outcomes, or learning opportunities and capacities – the child carries, in either latent or cumulative terms, the burden of failure to the next stage. This then adds to the deficit and reduces the probability of future success. This is what makes it imperative to reach the child at this critical early stage of life, and ensure that the child crosses each sub-stage of the development continuum successfully.

Wanted: A Concrete Indicator of Successful Child Development

How do we know a child in India is developing optimally? Indian research

---

[2] Amartya Sen 1999.

[3] Shore 1997.

and research elsewhere provide ample evidence today of the close links among the developmental aspects of good health, nutrition, psychosocial development and education. Given this synergistic relationship, *can the probability of the Indian child successfully completing primary schooling be used as a proxy indicator for the attributes of integrated child development?* The answer is yes, both as a significant milestone in the development continuum and as a concrete indicator of overall optimal child development.

Just as important, primary school completion is an indicator of enhanced life chances. Studies show how lifetime earnings go up with levels of education; indeed, some of this literature argues that primary school completion provides the greatest return on investment in education.[4] Primary education for children is important in itself. But it is also a critical part of any long-term strategy to develop human resources, sustain economic growth, alleviate poverty, and move closer to a strong and equitable rights-based democracy. Along with health and nutrition, early childhood

and primary education serve as the solid foundation on which lifelong development and learning can be built.

But then it becomes necessary to define "successful" completion of primary school. The term "successful" is significant. In the Indian context, the non-detention policy (which is being followed in most Indian states), means that children are generally promoted to the next grade regardless of actual learning levels.[5] As a result, children often go through the primary grades without even acquiring the basic competencies related to the 3 R's[6] (Reading, wRiting and aRithmetic) At the same time, "primary education" cannot be limited to literacy and numeracy skills. We need to define an ideal of all-round development, in terms of attributes for a healthy and educated child at the age of 11+years. These attributes have to enhance learning outcomes, physical and psychosocial development, and develop competencies that will enable the child to enter pre-adolescence with ease and confidence. The child should, in addition to learning literacy and numeracy skills, be able to

Successful completion of primary school indicates all-round development.

Box 1.1 : Rationale for the Proxy Indicator

◆ Investments in health, nutrition and ECD must display returns, which have to be measured with an index appropriate for India.

◆ The use of a common set of indicators by coordinating agencies and departments makes monitoring at each stage easier, and ensures effective multi-sectoral convergence.

◆ The conceptual framework derived from the indicators will guide further research, which in turn will inform policy and program inputs. This includes the effective use of resources and improved public-private partnerships at the community level.

---

[4] P. Duraiswamy 2000 and UNESCO/OECD 2002.

[5] Repetition, on the other hand, is the result of either low attendance level or the child's being underage for the next grade.

[6] NCERT 1998.

demonstrate active learning capacity, good health and nutrition, good habits/values, and above all, self-esteem.

Given this rationale, this report presents the milestone of successful completion of primary education as a proxy indicator of the successful development of the child and improved life chances (see Box 1.1). Such a holistic set of outcomes is the result, not just of educational inputs, but of the integrated composite of health, nutritional, and psychosocial inputs throughout the child's stages of development. This report begins with this basic premise, and builds a case for multi-sectoral interventions for holistic and integrated child development along the entire development continuum, from the prenatal stage to 11+ years, which is being considered the end of the childhood period.

The Indian Context: An Overview of Policies, Programs and the Current Situation

To put this proxy indicator to use in the Indian context, it would be useful to have an overview of what is the child population that is being addressed and what is the Indian child's situation today. The 347.5 million children in India below the age of 14 make up 33.8 percent of the country's total population. Of these, 49.3 percent are girls. Of the total child population, 6 percent are infants below the age of one, 12 percent are toddlers between 1-2 years, and 22.2 percent are pre-schoolers aged 3-5 years. 59.8 percent are in the age group of 6-14 years.

Given these numbers, what has been the role of policy framework and investment in the past decades? To begin with, the Constitution of India (1950) pledged that children would be given "opportunities and facilities to develop in a healthy manner and in conditions of freedom and dignity." With this sound starting point, India has, time and again, joined the community of nations in reaffirming global commitment to the cause of children. In 2002, for example, India was one of the UN member states to make a commitment to the Millennium Development Goals (MDG) (see Box 1.2).

Box 1.2 : A Global Commitment, a National Commitment

In the Special Session on Children in 2002, the UN member states committed themselves to promoting and protecting the rights of every child through national actions and international cooperation. The pledge was to promote healthy lives and quality education for children, and protect them against abuse, exploitation, violence, and HIV/AIDS.

India is a signatory to this world declaration, and the Tenth Five Year Plan has emphasized food and nutrition security, and reaching the child before the age of two. As a strategy, the Plan has included the institution of a National Charter for Children to ensure that "no child remains illiterate, hungry or lacks medical care" by the end of the Plan period. For this to happen, some of the Millennium Development Goals (MDG) identified are: reducing the under-5 mortality rate by two-thirds by 2015; ensuring universal primary education by 2015; and eliminating gender disparity in primary and secondary education by 2005.

Policies and programs for the Indian child:

The national intention has been in line with this global expression of commitment. In the last few decades, India has taken several policy and programmatic initiatives, specifically in the areas of health, education and nutrition. Building on the constitutional commitment to provide opportunities for education to children up to the age of 14 years (Article 45), the policy framework has been strengthened in recent times with the 86th Constitutional Amendment. This amendment has made basic education a fundamental right of every child from the age of 6 to 14 years and included, under Article 45, Early Childhood Care and Education (ECCE) as a constitutional provision for children below the age of six.

The government has also tried to address issues concerning children through specific policies – such as the National Policy for Children (1974), the National Policy on Education (1986/92), and the more recent ratification of the Convention on the Rights of the Child (1992). Acknowledging that malnutrition is a multifaceted problem that needs a multi-sectoral approach, the National Nutrition Policy was formulated in 1993, and a National Plan of Action initiated in 1995. The Tenth Five Year Plan (2002-2007) emphasizes food and nutrition security, beginning with children under two years of age. Its strategy includes setting up a National Charter for Children to ensure that "no child remains illiterate, hungry or lacks medical care" by the end of the Plan period.

In keeping with this policy framework, several schemes for children, sponsored by either the center or the state, are in place (Table 1.1). Existing schemes for children include such prominent programs as the Integrated Child Development Services (ICDS), the RCH Scheme, ECE or the *Balwadi* Programs, the Mid-day Meal Scheme (MMS), as well as formal and alternative (non-formal) primary education programs. Schemes that empower women to address poverty in a holistic way have also been set up.

Table 1.1 : Major Programs for Children from Conception to 11+ Years		
Programs for children, prenatal-3 years	**Programs for children, 3-6 years**	**Programs for children, 6-11 years**
Child Survival and Safe Motherhood (CSSM)	Integrated Child Development Services (ICDS)	*Sarva Shiksha Abhiyan* (SSA)
ICDS	Crèches and Day Care	District Primary Education Program (DPEP)
Reproductive and Child Health (RCH)	Early Childhood Education (ECE)	Teacher Education Scheme
Pradhan Mantri Gramodaya Yojana (PMGY) — nutrition support	Balwadis	Midday Meal Scheme (MMS)
National Programs for Blindness, goiter control		

Table 1.2 : Comparative Indicators for India, Developed and Developing Countries, 2002			
Programs for children, prenatal-3 years	**Developing Countries**	**Developed Countries**	**India**
Infant mortality rate (IMR) per 1000 live births	62	5	67
Under-5 mortality rate per 1000 live births	90	7	93
Percentage of infants with low birth weight (LBW) (1995-2000)	17	7	30
Percentage of children moderately & severely underweight (prenatal-4 years)	27	-	47
Wasting (12-23 months), moderate & severe (1995-2001)	10	-	16
Stunting (24-59 months), moderate & severe (1995-2001)	32	-	46
Percentage of one-year olds fully immunized for TB	81		81
Percentage of one-year olds fully immunized for Diphtheria, pertussis and tetanus (DPT)	73	95	70
Percentage of one-year olds fully immunized for polio	73	91	70
Percentage of one-year olds fully immunized for measles	73	90	67
Gross primary school enrollment ratio – Male	105	102	111
Gross primary school enrollment ratio – Female	96	102	92
Net primary school enrollment/attendance (percentage)	80	97	76
Net Primary school enrollment ratio – Male	84	96	78
Net Primary school enrollment ratio – Female	77	97	64
Percentage of Grade I enrollment reaching Grade 5 of primary school	79	-	68
Total percentage of children with access to safe water	78	100	84
Urban percentage of children with access to safe water	92	100	95
Rural percentage of children with access to safe water	69	100	79

Source: The State of the World's Children, UNICEF 2004

The evaluation of some of these programs on the ground indicates that there has been, at the very least, a fragmented impact. For instance, the ICDS, which was greatly expanded during the Eighth Plan period (1992-97), has had some impact on the incidence of severe malnutrition in children. Interventions with pregnant women and infants have also yielded significant results in the past. The EEC programs have had some positive impact on enrollment and retention in primary grades.[7] Though its influence on the nutritional status of primary school children has been minimal, the MMS has contributed to higher enrollment.[8] Again, several CSSs including DPEP have stimulated enrollment. But several of these positive results are accompanied by severe limitations:

• Levels of moderate to severe malnutrition and morbidity

---

[7] Kaul and Upadhyay 1994.

[8] UNICEF 1999.

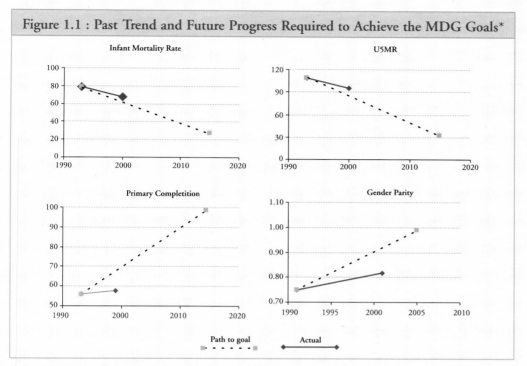

Figure 1.1 : Past Trend and Future Progress Required to Achieve the MDG Goals*

Note: MDG past and target figures are taken from Deolalikar (2003) MDG study

continue to constrain better life chances for more than half the child population.

- Even though schemes such as DPEP have helped increase enrollment levels, their impact on primary school completion and learning achievement is uneven.

- Evaluation studies reveal wide gaps between the conceptualization and actual implementation of programs. These include a lack of holistic planning and convergence among sectors, so that the impact of programs is limited.

So despite sound intentions and commitments, despite generally supportive policies and several programs in place, the situation of Indian children has not shown an improvement commensurate with the investments that have been made.

The situation of the Indian child – a dismal picture:

Indeed, the Indian child's situation continues to present a dismal picture. Table 1.2 clearly indicates that while India has made considerable progress over the baseline in ensuring child survival and basic education, the situation, in comparison with other developing countries and the more developed industrialized nations, is still not favorable. Unfavorable aspects include LBW, percentage of children severely or moderately underweight, wasting and stunting. Reaching the final primary grade is an important milestone for every child's development. But in spite of interventions over the years, almost 40 percent of the children who enroll in the first grade do not make it to even the fifth grade.

In the context of the MDGs, too, to which India is committed, progress in

The overall concern is why, despite supportive policies and significant investments, the development of the Indian child has been lagging behind in terms of global indicators.

India has been slower compared to other countries in the region. For instance, while Bangladesh and Nepal record a progress over the last decade (1990-2001) of 46.5 percent and 37.24 percent respectively in reduction in child mortality, India's progress is only 24.4 percent. A similar trend is seen on other indicators like gender equality and primary school completion. In terms of absolute levels also, for instance, while China's child mortality rate is 39 (in 2001) the corresponding rate for India is as high as 93, per thousand children. In terms of gender parity too, while China and Bangladesh are at 98 and 103 percent respectively, India is still at 78 percent. India's primary school completion rate too is only 76 percent as compared to China's 99 percent.[9] The prospects of attaining the MDG targets by 2015 thus seem doubtful, given this current pace. India's own Tenth Five Year Plan targets are more ambitious than the MDGs. As Figure 1.1 demonstrates, achieving the targets for each of the four MDG indicators itself poses a major challenge,

given the current pace. Achieving these may now require not only an acceleration of pace but also a possible change of track.

The writing on the wall:

Thus, the evidence is clear: the existing provisions for the Indian child need to be reviewed on a priority basis if national and international commitments are to be met. If the situation is to be reviewed afresh from the point of view of the child, and the way ahead determined, the need is to:

- identify the more critical outcomes and output indicators related to optimal development within each of the distinct sub-stages along the development continuum;

- prioritize these in terms of cost effectiveness and developmental significance; and

- link these to a coherent, coordinated network of services for the young child.

For a holistic impact, child development and early education has to be approached in a multi-sectoral and

---

Box 1.3 : The Rights-based Approach of the Tenth Five Year Plan

Emphasizes the "survival, protection and development" of children, especially of the girl child.

- Priority 1: Arrest declining sex ratio and address female feticide and infanticide to ensure "survival".

- Priority 2: Protect children in general, and children with special needs and in difficult circumstances, in particular.

- Priority 3: Promote development through health, nutrition and education -- through RCH and ICDS from conception to age two; the 6 service packages of ICDS for the pre-school age; and children of school-going age through various health, nutrition and educational programs.

---

9 Comparative data source: World Development Indicators, 2003.

integrated way. The Tenth Five Year Plan, in fact, is sensitive to this message – its rights-based approach has led to a discussion of holistic child development in addition to the section on separate sectors (see Box 1.3, particularly priority 3). The factors that determine Integrated Child Development (ICD) are not just in the classroom, or just in the primary school. They are part of a larger context and process. It is this process of development, with linked sub-stages, that this Report's conceptual framework addresses.

The Conceptual Framework
TOWARDS AN INTEGRATED APPROACH

The Conceptual Framework
Towards an Integrated Approach

Whether a child completes school successfully is not only determined by her development between the ages of 8-11, but also by what happened in each of the preceding stages — ages 6-8, 3-6, 1-3, and from conception to one month.

The Whole Child: The Empirical Basis

Current worldwide knowledge about child development, substantiated by Indian experience and research, clearly shows that the process of human development is continuous and cumulative. Each sub-stage of development necessarily influences development in the following stage/s, as well as for life. Ideally, a child should cross each sub-stage with success in all aspects of development. If the child fails to attain one or more of the desired developmental outcomes — whether related to health, nutrition or learning capacities – the burden is carried to the next stage. There the carried-over failure may lead to new failures being added to the child's baggage.

The factors that make up the whole context of the child's development encompass health, nutrition and education. Again, research illustrates that the relationship among these factors is synergistic, interdependent and complementary. For instance, learning capacity and motivation – crucial for school and lifelong learning – is adversely affected by nutritional and health deficits.[10] Children who receive psychosocial stimulation along with nutritional supplementation benefit more in terms of gain in nutritional status, compared to those who receive nutritional supplementation alone.[11] Indian researchers have also observed the negative impact of malnutrition on the cognitive and physical capacities of children, particularly in the first two years of life.[12]

Moreover, research indicates that the nature and extent of the impact of nutritional deficiency depends on the timing of the deficiency. The period from conception to the age of six years, especially the first three years, make up the critical periods for the development of important functions (see Figure 2.1). These include binocular vision, emotional control, habitual ways of responding, language and literacy, symbols and relative quality – all of which influence both school and lifelong learning and achievement.[13] For instance, iodine deficiency in utero has permanent effects on brain development, and most growth faltering occurs between 6-24 months. This vulnerable period sees the development of fundamental motor and cognitive skills, completion of the brain growth spurt,

The whole context of the child's development includes health, nutrition and education factors, and the relationship among these is synergistic, interdependent and complementary.

---

[10] Levinger 1994, Del Rosso and Marek 1996.

[11] Martorell 1997.

[12] Ghai 1975, Natesan and Devadas 1981, Anandalakshmi 1982, Bhattacharya 1981.

[13] Doherty 1997, Mustard 1999.

occurrence of physical growth failure, and high rates of infectious disease.[14]

Another crucial factor influencing the cognitive and psychosocial development of children, and their ability to adjust to and get the most of schooling, is derived from the "family-scaffolding" hypothesis. This hypothesis links longer-term effects of early childhood interventions with improvement in family situation and functioning.[15] Empirical evidence suggests the need to empower the family, particularly mothers, both as caregivers and from the socioeconomic point of view. This is vital to

optimize and sustain gains from child development interventions.

A Conceptual Framework for the Indian Child's Holistic Development

On the basis of a multi-sectoral review of current Indian as well as international knowledge, the basic developmental outcomes, outputs, indicators and determinants along the child development continuum from prenatal to 11+ years were identified. These provided the parameters for Indian ECD professionals to define a conceptual framework for the Indian child's development.[16] The basic guiding premise of this framework is that the Indian

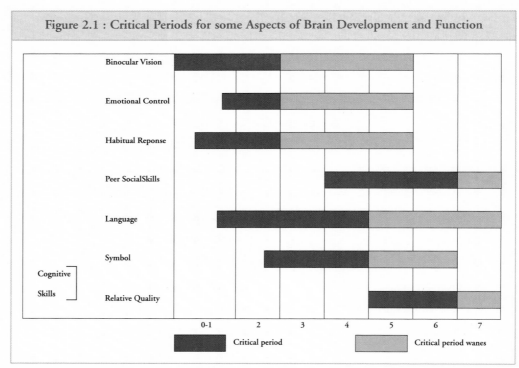

Figure 2.1 : Critical Periods for some Aspects of Brain Development and Function

Source: Adapted from Doherty 1997

---

[14] Lozoff 1990.

[15] Sternberg and Grigorenko 1997.

[16] The discussion of the Indian conceptual framework in this chapter is based on the research review "Integrated Child Development – A Conceptual Framework," New Concept Information Systems, New Delhi. The review was undertaken for this Report.

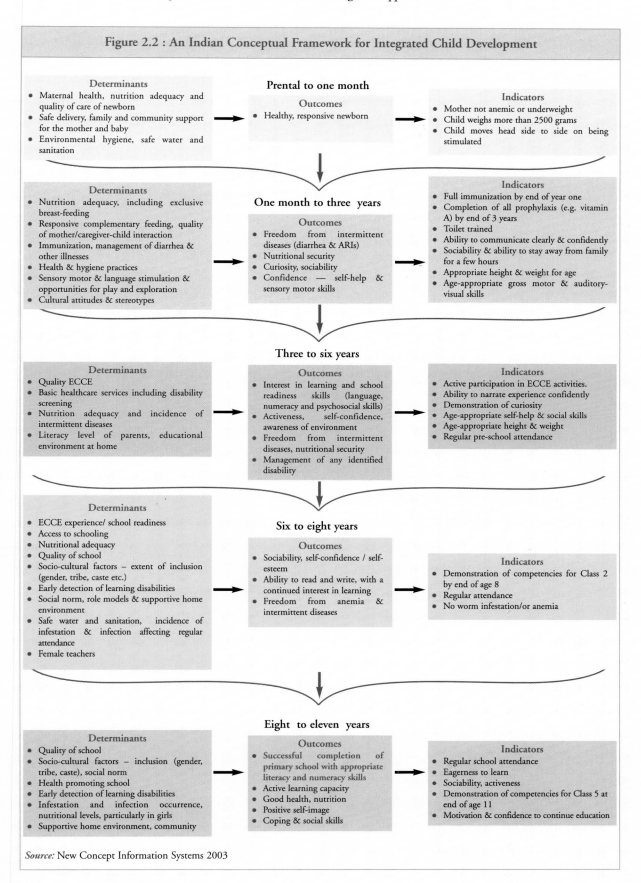

Figure 2.2 : An Indian Conceptual Framework for Integrated Child Development

Prental to one month

Determinants
- Maternal health, nutrition adequacy and quality of care of newborn
- Safe delivery, family and community support for the mother and baby
- Environmental hygiene, safe water and sanitation

Outcomes
- Healthy, responsive newborn

Indicators
- Mother not anemic or underweight
- Child weighs more than 2500 grams
- Child moves head side to side on being stimulated

One month to three years

Determinants
- Nutrition adequacy, including exclusive breast-feeding
- Responsive complementary feeding, quality of mother/caregiver-child interaction
- Immunization, management of diarrhea & other illnesses
- Health & hygiene practices
- Sensory motor & language stimulation & opportunities for play and exploration
- Cultural attitudes & stereotypes

Outcomes
- Freedom from intermittent diseases (diarrhea & ARIs)
- Nutritional security
- Curiosity, sociability
- Confidence — self-help & sensory motor skills

Indicators
- Full immunization by end of year one
- Completion of all prophylaxis (e.g. vitamin A) by end of 3 years
- Toilet trained
- Ability to communicate clearly & confidently
- Sociability & ability to stay away from family for a few hours
- Appropriate height & weight for age
- Age-appropriate gross motor & auditory-visual skills

Three to six years

Determinants
- Quality ECCE
- Basic healthcare services including disability screening
- Nutrition adequacy and incidence of intermittent diseases
- Literacy level of parents, educational environment at home

Outcomes
- Interest in learning and school readiness skills (language, numeracy and psychosocial skills)
- Activeness, self-confidence, awareness of environment
- Freedom from intermittent diseases, nutritional security
- Management of any identified disability

Indicators
- Active participation in ECCE activities.
- Ability to narrate experience confidently
- Demonstration of curiosity
- Age-appropriate self-help & social skills
- Age-appropriate height & weight
- Regular pre-school attendance

Six to eight years

Determinants
- ECCE experience/ school readiness
- Access to schooling
- Nutritional adequacy
- Quality of school
- Socio-cultural factors – extent of inclusion (gender, tribe, caste etc.)
- Early detection of learning disabilities
- Social norm, role models & supportive home environment
- Safe water and sanitation, incidence of infestation & infection affecting regular attendance
- Female teachers

Outcomes
- Sociability, self-confidence / self-esteem
- Ability to read and write, with a continued interest in learning
- Freedom from anemia & intermittent diseases

Indicators
- Demonstration of competencies for Class 2 by end of age 8
- Regular attendance
- No worm infestation/or anemia

Eight to eleven years

Determinants
- Quality of school
- Socio-cultural factors – inclusion (gender, tribe, caste), social norm
- Health promoting school
- Early detection of learning disabilities
- Infestation and infection occurrence, nutritional levels, particularly in girls
- Supportive home environment, community

Outcomes
- Successful completion of primary school with appropriate literacy and numeracy skills
- Active learning capacity
- Good health, nutrition
- Positive self-image
- Coping & social skills

Indicators
- Regular school attendance
- Eagerness to learn
- Sociability, activeness
- Demonstration of competencies for Class 5 at end of age 11
- Motivation & confidence to continue education

Source: New Concept Information Systems 2003

child's development requires an integrated and synergistic approach. Thus the framework presented by this report takes into account the needs of the whole child – from maternal health for prenatal security, to the weight of the newborn, to early nutrition, to psychosocial environment, to readiness for school and beyond. It encompasses the child's progress through a development continuum marked by a series of sub-stages of development – all of which have a cumulative impact on the child's development (see Figure 2.2), and on the probability of completing primary schooling successfully.

At each stage, the child's chances are influenced by a set of determinants. These determinants are complex, affecting outcomes individually as well as together. To assess outcomes, and predict the probability of reaching the goal of integrated development, measurable indicators are required, and specific development objectives and priorities have to be identified for each sub-stage of the child's development (see Figures 2.2 and 2.3). Equally, measurable indicators that affect outcomes need to be singled out. And these objectives and indicators need to be interlinked vertically, in terms of sub-stages, but also horizontally, across sectors.

Two-way Traffic: Determinants, Outcomes and Indicators
Sub-stage 1 (prenatal to one month):

This basic foundation period of development, indeed of survival, is influenced by a complex of determinants: maternal health (physical and emotional, including adequate nutritional intake of the expectant mother); safe delivery and care of the newborn; and family and community support, including hygiene, safe water and sanitation (see Figure 2.4). This is a sub-stage most critical for brain development.[17] A healthy pregnancy increases the likelihood of a full-term uncomplicated birth, normal birth weight and healthy brain development. The single largest factor placing babies at risk for poor development is LBW. The mother's education, age and emotional status also emerge as significant

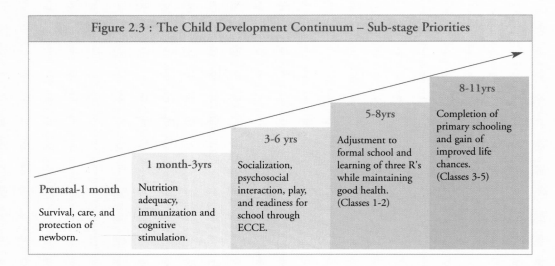

Figure 2.3 : The Child Development Continuum – Sub-stage Priorities

8-11yrs
Completion of primary schooling and gain of improved life chances. (Classes 3-5)

5-8yrs
Adjustment to formal school and learning of three R's while maintaining good health. (Classes 1-2)

3-6 yrs
Socialization, psychosocial interaction, play, and readiness for school through ECCE.

1 month-3yrs
Nutrition adequacy, immunization and cognitive stimulation.

Prenatal-1 month
Survival, care, and protection of newborn.

---

[17] McCain, Mustard et al 1999.

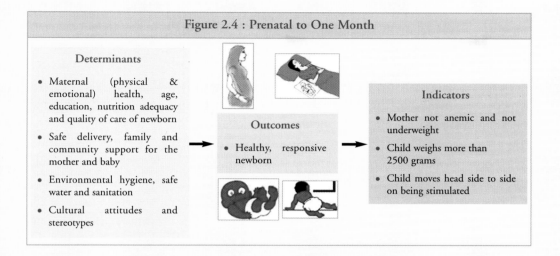

Figure 2.4 : Prenatal to One Month

Determinants

- Maternal (physical & emotional) health, age, education, nutrition adequacy and quality of care of newborn
- Safe delivery, family and community support for the mother and baby
- Environmental hygiene, safe water and sanitation
- Cultural attitudes and stereotypes

Outcomes

- Healthy, responsive newborn

Indicators

- Mother not anemic and not underweight
- Child weighs more than 2500 grams
- Child moves head side to side on being stimulated

factors. In the Indian context, the parental attitude and preference for a male child becomes the starting point of the gender bias in the family and in society at large. In fact, the survival of the girl child is a particularly relevant issue given the sex ratio in some Indian states in the 2001 Census.

Sub-stage 2 (one month to three years):

The mother's nutritional intake continues to be important for the growing child after birth (see Figure 2.5). A nutritionally adequate child would have been exclusively breastfed to begin with, and then provided timely, appropriate complementary feeding. Indian researchers have shown how malnutrition can hinder the cognitive and physical capacities of children, especially in the first two years of life.[18] These years are critical for brain development, and so extremely vulnerable to environmental influence; deprivation may, in fact, result in irreversible deficits. The quality of adult-child interactions and the child's cumulative experience during the first 18 months is likely to influence the process of brain

development. Immunization of both mother and child against communicable diseases, and immunizing the child against childhood illnesses, are also necessary during this period. All these needs grow in significance when applied to the Indian context, which, in contrast to the desirable scenario, is characterized by high under-five mortality rates, low female literacy rates, early marriage, the burden of sibling care, food security issues, malnutrition and lack of adequate health services.

Sub-stage 3 (three to six years):

This period continues to be significant for brain development and as a foundation for lifelong learning. If the child has negotiated the previous sub-stages successfully with the help of a conducive environment, the priority now shifts from an emphasis on nutritional and health needs to psychosocial development (see Figure 2.6). Crucial for all-round physical, cognitive, social and emotional development of the child, 50 percent of an individual's cognitive development takes place by the time the child is 5-6 years old.[19] Similarly, the most

---

[18] Ghai 1975, Natesan and Devadas 1981, Bhattacharya 1981, Anandalakshmi 1982.

[19] Bloom 1964.

important forms of social and emotional behavior that may appear at this stage are cooperative play, formation of personal and social habits, desire for social approval and appreciation, preferably through physical touch, imitation and role modeling, and the desire to communicate, often with imagination. Good quality early childhood care and education (ECCE) becomes an indispensable intervention, particularly for children from disadvantaged families (see Box 2.1).

What the child needs to learn during this period – from planned cognitive language and creative activity, to motor skills, to developing good habits of health and hygiene – can all be inculcated using play as the medium.[20] In the Indian context, the child in the 4-6 age group also needs specific cognitive, social and psychomotor experiences that will promote her school readiness – prepare her better for entering school and adjusting to its demands. The child, particularly a first generation learner, needs help to develop the necessary reading, writing and mathematical readiness skills. Most of all, the child needs to develop an interest in learning so as to successfully negotiate the primary school curriculum. ECCE programs have demonstrated the significant impact they can have on the achievement of these outcomes, both in India and elsewhere. In India, they have also helped the participation of girls in

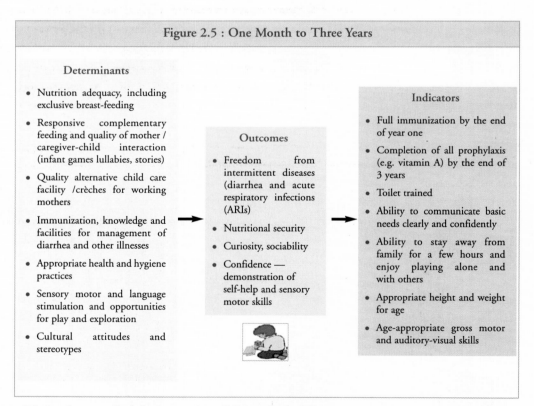

Figure 2.5 : One Month to Three Years

Determinants

- Nutrition adequacy, including exclusive breast-feeding
- Responsive complementary feeding and quality of mother / caregiver-child interaction (infant games lullabies, stories)
- Quality alternative child care facility /crèches for working mothers
- Immunization, knowledge and facilities for management of diarrhea and other illnesses
- Appropriate health and hygiene practices
- Sensory motor and language stimulation and opportunities for play and exploration
- Cultural attitudes and stereotypes

Outcomes

- Freedom from intermittent diseases (diarrhea and acute respiratory infections (ARIs)
- Nutritional security
- Curiosity, sociability
- Confidence — demonstration of self-help and sensory motor skills

Indicators

- Full immunization by the end of year one
- Completion of all prophylaxis (e.g. vitamin A) by the end of 3 years
- Toilet trained
- Ability to communicate basic needs clearly and confidently
- Ability to stay away from family for a few hours and enjoy playing alone and with others
- Appropriate height and weight for age
- Age-appropriate gross motor and auditory-visual skills

"The first three years offer us the chance to change the life course of a child."
Source: Young 1997

---

[20] Kaul 1989, 1992; Swaminathan 1990; Consultative Group on ECCD, 2000.

Box 2.1 : Readiness for School, Readiness for Life

◆ ECCE programs can contribute to better nutrition and health, and better rates of school enrollment (Myers 1995; A study of about 33,000 children across 8 Indian states shows a significant impact on retention (estimated to increase by 15-20 percent) in primary grades. Kaul et al 1994).

◆ Readiness for reading, counting and social interaction is directly influenced by the pre-school experiences of the child. Since there is a strong link between the quality of ECD and learning competencies (Swaminathan 1990), active learning that leads to perceptual and motor skills is the key to developing the child's learning abilities.

◆ Longitudinal research in India and elsewhere has endorsed the significant impact of good quality, process based ECCE curriculum on mathematics learning in later years (Kaul et al 1996).

---

schooling by releasing them from the responsibility of sibling care. This is particularly true if the ECCE center is located near, or in the primary school and has timings synchronized with those of the school. Given these benefits, ECCE facilities need to be expanded substantially. This sub-stage is also important from the perspective of early identification of disabilities and planning for its management.

With increased exposure to the environment, the child's vulnerability to worm infestation and intermittent illnesses also increases during this sub-stage. As a result, certain systemic needs arise in addition to the need for safe water. These needs include appropriate support from healthcare systems such as sanitation, and access to primary health centers (PHCs), *anganwadi centers* (AWC) and non-governmental organizations (NGOs), for nutritional support and immunization against communicable diseases. At the same time, increased activity calls for a higher energy requirement and the appropriate

---

Figure 2.6 : Three to Six Years

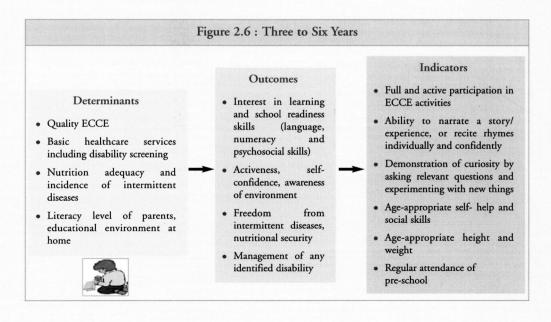

Determinants

- Quality ECCE
- Basic healthcare services including disability screening
- Nutrition adequacy and incidence of intermittent diseases
- Literacy level of parents, educational environment at home

Outcomes

- Interest in learning and school readiness skills (language, numeracy and psychosocial skills)
- Activeness, self-confidence, awareness of environment
- Freedom from intermittent diseases, nutritional security
- Management of any identified disability

Indicators

- Full and active participation in ECCE activities
- Ability to narrate a story/ experience, or recite rhymes individually and confidently
- Demonstration of curiosity by asking relevant questions and experimenting with new things
- Age-appropriate self- help and social skills
- Age-appropriate height and weight
- Regular attendance of pre-school

enhancement of nutrition and nutrition adequacy. Hence a nutritious meal during the pre-school hours is a desirable intervention. Research indicates the link between nutritional supplementation, and improved cognitive development and school attainment. A study that placed 1000 LBW premature babies in enriched daycare centers between 12-36 months found that the poorest children with the least educated mothers gained the most.[21]

Sub-stage 4 (six to eight years):

This is the primary school stage, the first of two developmental sub-stages (6-8 and 8-11 years) linked to primary education.

The 6-8 year period is an extension of the early childhood stage, where play is a dominant need as well as an effective means of learning (Figure 2.7). The child is also in transition as far as cognitive development is concerned – moving towards more logical and analytical thinking and reasoning. As in the previous sub-stage, the incidence of minor infective diseases increases with exposure to the general environment. Nutritional demands match high growth demands, and influence the learning capacity of the child, hence a cooked mid-day meal as in pre-school continues to be desirable.

Figure 2.7 : Six to Eight Years

Determinants	Outcomes	Indicators
• ECCE experience/ school readiness	• Freedom from anemia and intermittent diseases	• Demonstration of competencies for Class 2 by the end of age 8
• Access to schooling	• Sociability, self-confidence/ self-esteem	• Regular attendance
• Food and nutritional adequacy, midday meal in school	• Ability to read and write, with a continued interest in learning	• No worm infestation or anemia
• Quality of school (physical inputs, instructional materials, use of home language, teacher quality and behavior, school climate, number of instructional days, daily time on task)		
• Socio-cultural factors – extent of inclusion (gender, tribe, caste, etc.)		
• Early detection of learning disabilities (school health)		
• Social norm, role models & supportive home environment (economic status, child labor, migration)		
• Appreciation and success experiences		
• Safe water and sanitation, food adequacy, incidence of infestation and infection affecting regular attendance		
• Female teachers		

Are our schools ready for children?

The 1999 PROBE survey makes it clear that the quality of the school is important to retain children in school. Incentives such as the midday meal, free uniforms and textbooks become necessary only if the quality of schooling is not good enough to influence demand.

---

[21] Young 2000.

This sub-stage has been especially carved out of the primary education stage since it requires specific attention in the Indian context. It is an important stage to help children learn and master the basic skills of reading, writing and arithmetic, leading to the development of learning skills and a positive self-concept. But the data indicates that this sub-stage is characterized by the highest dropout level across the country, particularly among the large majority of children who come to primary school without an ECCE background. This finding makes the sub-stage especially vulnerable for primary school completion, with the vulnerability heightened in the case of girl children. Large enrollments in the first two grades, coupled with the lack of teachers as well as multi-grade classroom situations, lead to a situation where children remain unengaged in any meaningful activity for long hours. The consequence is that children are "pushed out" of an uninteresting and unchallenging classroom situation.[22] The lack of a community norm of sending children to school can also affect retention.[23] All these can be contributing factors, and they need specific and contextual examination in view of the number of dropouts at this stage.

Sub-stage 5 (eight to eleven years):

Further along the development continuum, the 8-11 year age group tends to demonstrate a greater capacity for logical thinking, and for more structured

---

Figure 2.8 : Eight to Eleven Years

Determinants	Outcomes	Indicators
• Quality of school (comprehensive curriculum, physical inputs, instructional material, familiarity with school language, teacher quality and teaching-learning practices, school climate, number of instructional days, time on task , continuous & comprehensive assessment)	• Successful completion of primary school with appropriate literacy and numeracy skills	• Regularity in school attendance
• Socio-cultural factors – inclusion (gender, tribe, caste etc.) and social norm	• Active learning capacity	• Eagerness to learn
• Health promoting school	• Good health and nutrition	• Sociability and activeness
• Early detection of learning disabilities	• Positive self-image and set of values	• Demonstration of competencies for Class 5 at the end of age 11
• Supportive home environment (economic environment, migration, child labor, domestic chores)	• Coping skills and social competencies	• Motivation and confidence as to continuing education in upper primary grades
• Appreciation and success experiences		
• Food adequacy, infestation and infection occurrence, nutritional levels, particularly in girls		

"Successfully" completes primary education

---

[22] Ramachandran 2003b, Kaul et al 2003

[23] Jha and Jhingran 2002.

and formal learning. The child has an increased attention span and is able to persevere on a given learning task if it is of interest to the child (Figure 2.8). Gender issues begin to surface around this age, and girls face the risk of dropping out of school because of domestic responsibilities. But easy access to school can offset this risk of the girl not being able to complete school.

Again, this is the stage when child labor, and the general phenomenon of the working child, surfaces and starts to take shape, affecting school attendance and completion. The opportunity cost of schooling also becomes a potent factor in determining the probability of a child completing primary school. The nature of the curriculum, the costs of schooling, the physical and pedagogical school inputs including time on task, teacher quality, classroom pedagogy and organization, school management, and academic climate – all these emerge as significant determinants.[24] As before, nutritional and health needs continue to be significant. Common nutritional deficiencies include iron deficiency anemia, Vitamin-A, protein calorie malnutrition and iodine deficiency. Worm infestations and malaria due to poor sanitation aggravate anemia; these deficiencies reduce energy levels, and make children more vulnerable to intermittent illnesses, in turn affecting their school attendance and achievement.

The Concentric Interaction within the Framework Mosaic

The research review reveals the complex and concentric system of relationships among determinants that act interactively on the child. Figure 2.9 illustrates the influence of the immediate and surrounding environment emerging from the review. The basic, underlying, and immediate conditions around the child influence the child's integrated development. Immediate concerns relate to the mother, caregiver and family; and these relations are bi-directional and reciprocal. If the immediate caregiver relates to the child in an open and interactive way, the child will be equally responsive. The immediate caregiver/family response can be either enhanced or undermined by conditions within the family, and by conditions outside acting on the family. For instance, the family's relationship with the neighborhood, and the presence or absence of daycare and its quality, can affect the child in different ways. The mother's education and employment, and the family's economic situation, are crucial factors.

Beyond this intimate neighborhood circle is the larger system – comprising health services, environmental sanitation, and work environment for instance – that influences the development of the child. For example, women engaged in agriculture in rural areas face work situations different from their counterparts in urban areas, who may not have flexible timings. Factors such as these in turn affect the quantity and quality of care provided to the child.

The largest circle is the general cultural and social environment, which either reinforces or erodes values, customs and

---

[24] Fuller and Clarke 1994, Lockheed and Verspoor 1991

practices. Is there a social norm for children going to school, and then going ahead to complete school? Is there a social norm of washing hands before meals and keeping drinking water covered? Is there a social norm of institutional delivery? Questions such as these become very significant in the attempt to change attitudes and behavior in any given community. Within and between each circle, there is dynamic movement. As a result, development is not static. Moreover, there is no single driving force. What is closer to the reality is a combination of ripple and spiral effects.

We have seen that the interaction of the factors involved in child development is complex, and that the resulting conceptual framework is like a mosaic. The next step is a close-up view of ground realities within the parameters provided by this framework. In other words, we need to answer the central question: where is the Indian child today?

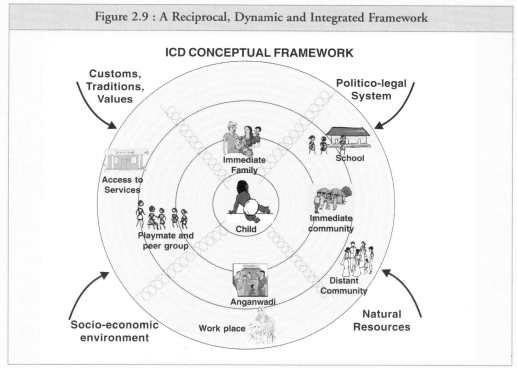

Figure 2.9 : A Reciprocal, Dynamic and Integrated Framework

Source: New Concept Information Systems, 2003

The Real Picture
THE STATUS OF
THE INDIAN CHILD

The Real Picture

The Status of the Indian Child

The Real Pictures, Frame by Frame

Where is the Indian child from the poorer households today? In, for example, a stark field picture of a poverty-stricken rural tribal household. There were four children in the household – and all of them were fighting over raw custard apples, which seemed to be the only main meal of the morning. The mother made pretence of getting ready to cook but did not light the *chulha* (stove). Finally, she gave a fistful of leftover rice to her son before he left for school. He ate this with some *ganji* (gruel) he brought from the neighbor's house.

Again, the Indian child is to be found in Kamla, the "very responsible" dropout. Kamla, who lives in the Sitapur District of Uttar Pradesh, was a regular student and enjoyed being in the village government public school. But at eleven years of age, she is now doing "what she will use in her future life." Though there are other adults in the family who can handle the task, Kamla is out of school so she can run her not-so-old grandmother's household. Kamla, healthy and motivated to learn, has to be content with the old neighbor's compliment: "She is a very responsible girl…"[25]

The first household's main meal and Kamla's loss of her right to education are just two grim reminders of the "chances at

development" so many Indian children miss out on. And these two individual pictures need to be multiplied a very large number of times to understand the magnitude of the current situation. It is not just a few unlucky children we are talking of, but significant numbers of the 347.5 million children in India below the age of 14.[26] Large numbers of these future citizens live lives of hunger; even if there is something to eat, it is not enough, or not the right kind of food needed for a growing body and mind in the process of formation for life. Hunger and malnutrition place these children at a disadvantage early in life. More deprivation follows, with the children more vulnerable to disease, or to discrimination because of gender or caste, or to lack of family and community support. These children's chances at development are not determined just by their family's low income; their chances are also influenced by their immediate and larger environment – the primary caregiver, the parents; the family, the neighborhood, the community. Kamla and her hungry friends in the tribal household are a part of the larger situation of the Indian child in poverty settings

"The children observed have little to eat… the majority in poor households appeared malnourished and were pot-bellied with extremely thin limbs. Though they seemed active and alert, the effects of poor nutrition are likely to manifest themselves later in life."

Ramachandran et al 2003

Key indicators of the Indian child's current situation include health and nutrition, living conditions, psycho-social and cognitive development, enrollment in school, increased choices and opportunities, and ability for lifelong learning.

---

[25] Both examples are from Ramachandran et al 2003.

[26] 2001 Census figures, see GOI 2001b.

today, whether in rural habitations or urban slums – a situation that has to be measured in terms of certain key indicators: health and nutrition, living conditions, psychosocial and cognitive development, enrollment in school, increased choices and opportunities, and ability for lifelong learning.

The child's development is, as discussed earlier, a multi-sectoral topic of research. And given the complex interactive factors enabling, or hindering the child's development, this report makes use of both quantitative and qualitative data. Both types of data have to be viewed as linked sets of insights and information that inform each other, while making up, together, a multi-dimensional, composite picture of the child's world. Only then can we aim for a full picture of the Indian child today.

Has nothing been done for the Indian child? As a matter of fact, India has, in the last fifty years, made significant progress in fulfilling her children's right to survival and development. There has been, for instance, a sharp decline in childhood mortality from 242 deaths per 1000 births in 1960 to 93 in 2002, and in the incidence of Vaccine Preventable Diseases (VPDs), especially in neonatal tetanus and polio. ICDS have been expanded to improve access to ECD interventions for children from conception to the age of six years. Significant progress has also been made in universalizing access to primary education with, for instance, total enrollment at primary stage increasing from 97 million in 1990 to 114 million in 2000-01. The relative share of girls'

participation has also increased from 28.1 percent in 1950-51 to 43.7 percent in 2000-01 (Source: EFA National Plan for Action: India 2003). To some extent, progress has also been there in improving the quality of the content and process of teaching and learning. But despite these gains, the overall picture can by no means be considered satisfactory. A large number of children continue to "live in economic and social environments which impede their physical and mental development. These conditions include poverty, poor environmental sanitation, disease, infection, inadequate access to primary healthcare, inappropriate child caring and feeding practices.[27]"

Tracing the Child's Current Situation along the Continuum

Sub-stage 1 (prenatal to one month):

Maternal health:

Even before a child is visible in the picture, his or her chances of a healthy, happy life are being determined by the mother's overall health, effected particularly by her nutrition, her age at marriage and delivery, the spacing of her pregnancies and her weight. If the mother is malnourished and/or anemic, the child's weight at birth – an important factor for her survival and growth – is affected. The younger the delivering mother is, and the lower her age at marriage, the lower the chances of safe delivery of a healthy infant. And if the spacing between her pregnancies is too brief, her poor health may tell on the infant she delivers.

---

[27] Annual Report 1998-99, DWCD, GOI 1999b.

The ideal candidate for a pregnant woman and a delivering mother is, then, someone who has not got married or got pregnant too young; someone whose pregnancies have been spaced out; someone who has some education, and has awareness about antenatal care and nutrition practices. Keeping this ideal in mind, what are the findings about the mothers who actually contribute the first foundation for the Indian child's well being? The findings do not make for very good news. To begin with, most of the women interviewed were thin, anemic and had poor nutrition. And they had a very low level of awareness of nutrition during pregnancy, immunization and antenatal care.[28] The case studies in Andhra Pradesh, Karnataka and Uttar Pradesh revealed a disturbing trend among poor women – many deliberately eat less during pregnancy, believing this would mean smaller babies and easier (home) deliveries. The quantitative figures were equally worrying:

- The mean age at marriage in the households profiled was 13, 15 and 15 years respectively in the states of Andhra Pradesh, Karnataka, and Uttar Pradesh. These were much lower than the respective state averages of 18, 20 and 19 years.

- The high workload, more so in the case of women engaged in daily wage labor, gender bias, and the lack of family, community and institutional support, increase the expectant mother's vulnerability.

- One third of the mothers (35.8 percent) surveyed were underweight at the time of delivery, the problem being more acute among rural and Scheduled Caste (SC) women. The difference between the highest and lowest income quintiles in the urban areas was sharper than in the rural areas, suggesting the need to address urban poverty more specifically.

- Anemia in women is widely prevalent and more than 30 percent mothers were found to be anemic at childbirth. Moreover, northern states of Bihar, Rajasthan and Uttar Pradesh show percentages of anemic mothers going over 50 percent (see Figure 3.1).

- Overall, 40 percent of women were reported to be not taking iron folic tablets during pregnancy; the situation was severe among rural and tribal women.[29] Inter-state comparisons again indicate that the problem is more acute in the northern states of Bihar, Rajasthan and Uttar Pradesh.

Maternal health thus emerges as the most important factor to ensure optimal child development; and the nutrition of pregnant women, indeed of adolescent girls as well from a lifecycle perspective, emerges as a key policy priority.

Safe delivery:

The next critical step is a safe delivery by trained attendants. But despite various programs promoting institutional delivery or delivery by trained attendants, the case studies report that the majority of deliveries take place at home across the three states of

---

[28] Ramachandran et al 2003.

[29] Indicus Analytics 2003.

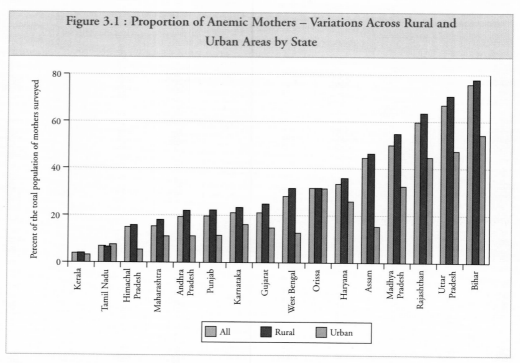

Figure 3.1 : Proportion of Anemic Mothers – Variations Across Rural and Urban Areas by State

Source: Indicus Analytics 2003 - Analysis of NFHS 1998-99

Andhra Pradesh, Karnataka and Uttar Pradesh. Delivery in these cases was assisted by a *dai* (traditional birth attendant) or a relative or a neighbor. Poor environmental hygiene, lack of safe water and poor sanitation also affected the safety of these home deliveries. Across the country too, only one third of deliveries from all economic classes are institutional,[30] and families did not even think it important to access trained midwives – auxiliary nurse midwives (ANMs).

In the context of child delivery, there is an important gender issue as well. While overall child survival is no longer a major issue, the survival of the girl child or the female foetus still causes concern. The sex ratio has dipped at the national level from 945 in 1991 to 927 in 2001 for the 0-6 age group. Surprisingly, the more prosperous states of Haryana, Gujarat, Maharashtra and Punjab demonstrate the lowest ratios (see Table 3.1). Also, consistently across the states, urban figures are lower than rural figures, clearly reflecting the need to focus on urban contexts on a priority basis.[31]

Birth weight:

The natural next question is about the infant's weight at birth. That this is an important issue is evident: one third of all births in the country are below the minimum acceptable birth weight of 2500gms. This is not surprising – given inadequate nutrition during pregnancy, and a general low level of awareness about

---

[30] NFHS data, see IIPS 2000b.

[31] One possible reason that needs further examination is easier access to technologies for sex determination in urban areas, despite efforts to regulate their use.

Table 3.1 : Urban and Rural Sex Ratios in some Relatively Prosperous States, 2001		
State	Urban	Rural
Haryana	784	795
Gujarat	809	824
Maharashtra	827	905
Punjab	908	923

Source: The State of the World's Children, UNICEF 2004

antenatal care or immunization (despite the presence of the *anganwadi* worker *(AWW)* and monthly visits by the auxiliary nurse midwife (ANM)). Significantly, the problem is most acute and concentrated in the central and northern part of the country, which is also the low female literacy belt (see Figure 3.2). The conclusion that can be drawn then is that a differentiated and need-based approach to interventions is required.

The social reality is that low literacy, poor health and nutritional status, all concomitants of poverty, contribute to poor fetal growth in pregnancy. This poor beginning for the child – the cumulative effects of poor maternal health, unsafe delivery, and the child's low birth weight – can only hinder the child's chances at the next sub-stage of development (one month to three years).

Sub-stage 2 (one month to three years):

From what we have seen in the first sub-stage, it follows that the child's nutrition in the next sub-stage continues to be of critical

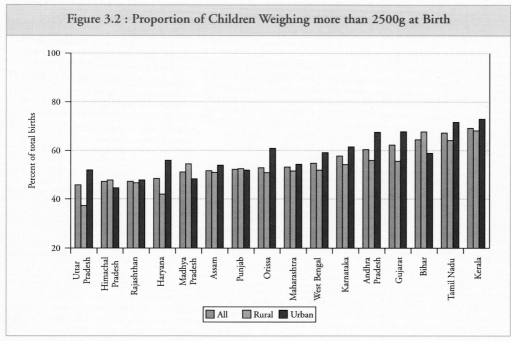

Figure 3.2 : Proportion of Children Weighing more than 2500g at Birth

Source: Indicus Analytics 2003 - Analysis of NFHS 1998-99

Conception to One Month: Findings and Priorities for Action	
Findings	**Priorities**
Maternal health poor: one-third underweight at time of delivery; widespread anemia; 40 percent not taking folic acid.	Antenatal care, including better nutrition for expectant mothers.
Nearly all deliveries at home, sometimes without trained attendants or environmental hygiene.	Institutional deliveries / better coverage by ANMs.
30 percent newborns have LBW.	
Gender issue: overall decreasing sex ratio, lower ratios in more prosperous states and urban areas.	Increasing awareness and community support through Information, Education, Communication (IEC): health and nutrition needs and practices during pregnancy; the advantages of increasing age at marriage, overcoming gender bias in family and community.

Pregnant and lactating mothers in Karnataka and Andhra Pradesh visited the anganwadi center, but this was not true of even a single woman surveyed in Uttar Pradesh. Most two-year olds were still being breast-fed in the three states. The mothers said they did not give the children any special weaning food.

importance, particularly since this is the critical stage for brain development and also the stage when the child is "at risk of growth faltering." Inadequate or inappropriate feeding practices, repeated episodes of acute infections, poor access to healthcare and general neglect, cause a substantial proportion of children to become moderately or severely malnourished by the age of 6-18 months. Though the IMR has declined considerably between 1960 and 2001 in India, the problem is still far from solved, particularly in terms of morbidity and malnutrition. But it is clear that improving the child's nutrition, and an increase in prenatal coverage, can reduce infant mortality.

Weight for age:

The child's weight for his/her age is an obvious indicator of his/her chances at survival, and his/her development in terms of health and nutrition. An examination of age-appropriate weight among Indian children between the ages of one month to three years shows that about 17 percent of children were underweight as against 30 percent at birth. Again, the children in the rural areas are worse off and of these more particularly are the ones in the lowest income quintile.[32] Across the three states in which case studies were carried out, children of this age in poor homes were observed to be getting inadequate supplemental nutrition, although most of them still acquire the appropriate developmental milestones for their age.[33]

What are some of the factors that make for an acceptable weight of the child? Besides the maternal factors discussed in the last section, other factors include smaller families and an adequate period of

[32] Indicus Analytics 2003.

[33] Ramachandran et al 2003

breastfeeding, and in addition, responsive feeding and care as the infant grows. The case studies observed that children in all the three states were being breast-fed almost up to two years, but were getting very little extra food. The problem was not just the availability of grains or fat and cooking oil; it was also that mothers had very little time to prepare separate food for the child.[34]

Immunization:

What else does the child desperately need at this stage? The child is vulnerable to VPDs, particularly if already poorly nourished, and living in surroundings with poor hygiene and sanitation. So in addition to sound nutrition, complete immunization and Vitamin A supplements during this period are critical for the child's future development. How close does the reality come to meeting these requirements?

- Despite regular immunization programs, over 50 percent of the one-year-old children in the country were not fully immunized; they had not received vaccination against measles and DPT, or three doses of the polio vaccine (see Figure 3.3). This observation was supported by the case studies as well. The differences between the highest and the lowest income quintiles was found to be more striking in urban areas; and in the case of social groups, immunization rates were the lowest among the tribals.

- As for the two-year-old children receiving Vitamin-A supplements, the situation was worse than that for immunization. Despite an increase in the number of children receiving Vitamin-A, about two-thirds had still

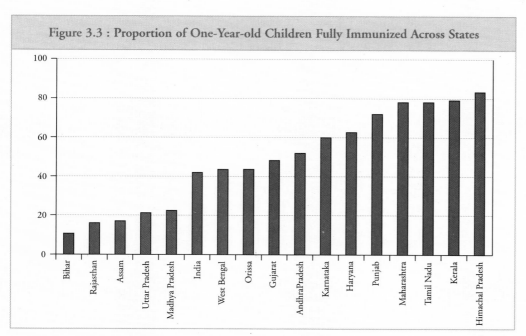

Figure 3.3 : Proportion of One-Year-old Children Fully Immunized Across States

Source: Indicus Analytics 2003 – Analysis of NFHS 1998-99

---

[34] Ibid.

not received it. Again, there were wide disparities among states, with Assam, Bihar, Rajasthan, Tamil Nadu and Uttar Pradesh performing the most poorly (see Figure 3.4). Overall, the lower castes, rural children and females tended to have much lower levels of Vitamin-A supplementation. This places these groups in the high-risk category for growth faltering.

Nutritional security:

On the whole, a significant number of children below the age of three years were found to suffer from endemic malnutrition. They were only partially immunized; and a good number suffered from infections, scabies, boils or rashes, considering the lack of sanitation and hygiene in their surroundings, although there was no shortage of water. The case studies report that children were found to suffer from intermittent illnesses such as colds, measles

and diarrhea. Interestingly, the local shops in the villages stocked antibiotics and sulpha drugs that they dispensed over the counter. Even small babies were given powdered drugs such as Septran and Novalgin dissolved in water. Also, with the increasing popularity of injections and allopathic medicines in both rural and urban areas, the poor seemed to have lost faith in traditional medicine. On the one hand, there is this evidence of a shift from traditional to modern medicines, but on the other, this changing perception is not accompanied by a greater awareness of sound health and medical practices. This is among the gaps and contradictions that the IEC needs to address.

While most children in the case studies were found to be malnourished, they had achieved appropriate milestones for their age, such as crawling, walking, running, and communicating their needs. In

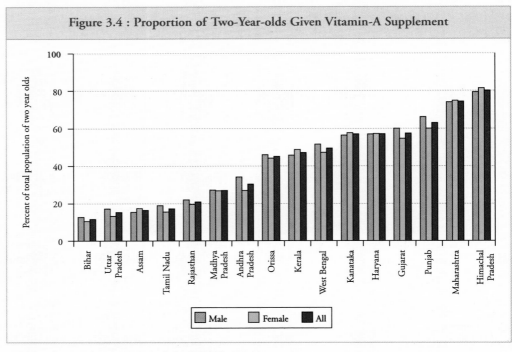

Figure 3.4 : Proportion of Two-Year-olds Given Vitamin-A Supplement

Source: Indicus Analytics 2003 – Analysis of NFHS 1998-99

Box 3.1 : Malnutrition: Causes and Pattern of Prevalence

♦ The prevalence of malnutrition among the under-threes is the highest in tribal blocks, followed by the rural and urban blocks, indicating the need for better targeting of services on a need basis.

Malnutrition is caused by

Proximal factors:

♦ Inadequate caring practices

♦ Low nutrient intake

♦ Illness (diarrhea/ pneumonia)

♦ Low birth weight

Distal factors:

♦ Poverty

♦ Lack of parents' education

♦ Poor adolescent and maternal nutritional status (intergenerational)

♦ Gender discrimination

♦ Low median age of woman at first birth.

Source: World Bank 1998a.

One Month to Three Years : Findings and Priorities for Action	
Findings	Priorities
30 percent of newborns have LBW; 17 percent are underweight; weight for age a bigger problem among rural and poor children.	Adequate breastfeeding, responsive feeding and care, supplemental nutrition.
Lactating mothers' visit AWC in Andhra Pradesh and Karnataka but not in Uttar Pradesh	Promoting visits of lactating mothers to AWC in all states.
Over 50 percent of one-year olds in the country not completely immunized; lower rates among tribals and urban poor.	
Two-thirds of two-year olds not received Vitamin-A supplement; lower caste and rural children, girls, poor urban children and children from some states placed at high risk for growth faltering.	Extend immunization and Vitamin A coverage with better targeting of the vulnerable.
Significant endemic malnutrition among the under 3-year olds.	Nutritional support and increasing awareness of better childcare and feeding practices.
Lack of sanitation and hygiene leading to intermittent illnesses and infections.	Bridging of gap between use of modern medicines and lack of awareness of safe health practices, while balancing this with revival of effective traditional medicine/medicinal practices.
Sibling interaction but little adult-child interaction.	Revival and dissemination of traditional interaction practices (stories, lullabies and infant games).

terms of psychosocial stimulation, there was little by way of adult-child interaction. However, continuous interaction with siblings and other children provided some opportunity for communicative and social stimulation, though this was still a long way off from the optimal level.

Sub-stage 3 (three to six years):
Health, hygiene and nutrition

It is not just infant mortality that is of concern; the risk to the child's survival continues into the next stage as well. Nutrition and immunization along with psychosocial stimulation influence the child's chances at survival, and improve the child's quality of life and preparation for the next stage. Equally important are health and hygiene. What sort of water, for example, does the child's household have access to? What about sanitation? Do the children develop sound personal habits? In answer, the field facts are:

- The mortality rate for the under-five age group was high in all the three states in which case studies were carried out.

- Majority of houses got drinking water from tube wells and protected water supply schemes, but the incidence of water-borne diseases was still high. Although there was no shortage of water, water storage and dispensing practices left much to be desired.

- Poor sanitation and unhygienic surroundings were found to lead to frequent bouts of diarrhea and other communicable diseases.

- The majority of the children observed in poor households appeared moderately to severely malnourished and were pot bellied with extremely thin limbs. While the researchers report that the children appeared active and alert, the latent and cumulative impact of their nutritional status on subsequent development and learning cannot but be a matter of concern.

Early childhood education:

In a fundamental way, health, nutrition, and poverty-related issues, such as short-term hunger and vulnerability to infections and childhood diseases, continue to be important. But the child's most important foundation blocks should be in place by this stage; and from the age of three onwards, the central focus for the child's development should shift to psychosocial development through a well planned, play-based and developmentally appropriate ECCE program. In terms of psychosocial development, one of the indicators is the level of readiness for primary school at the stage of entry. If the child is not adequately nourished, or completely immunized, or exposed to pre-schooling to profit from cognitive stimulation, the child's readiness for primary school – the milestone for this sub-stage – will be adversely affected. Interaction with primary teachers endorses the view that children not exposed to an organized pre-school program find it difficult to adjust to the school situation at the age of six years. Indian research has clearly demonstrated that participation in pre-schooling can make a positive difference of almost 15-20 percent in subsequent continuation in the primary grades, thus reducing the risk of dropouts. This is particularly true for the first-generation learners.[35] This is what the Indian child needs. But what does the data show?

On an average, only about 15 percent of children in this age group availed of some kind of pre-schooling, although almost 25 percent were enrolled in states such as Kerala, Maharashtra, Punjab and Tamil Nadu (see Figure 3.5). The proportion of children in pre-school in the urban areas was significantly higher than in the rural areas, possibly because of of private nurseries and preparatory schools in towns and cities which tend to serve as downward extensions of primary schools and are of doubtful quality. While ICDS, the major

program for children in this age group, has pre-school education as one of its six components, its quality remains a major concern. The case studies report this component to be almost non-existent in Andhra Pradesh and Uttar Pradesh, and of very poor quality in Karnataka, barring one center where the worker was exceptionally motivated. Predictably then, a recent study conducted in four regions (by Regional Institutes of Education in Ajmer, Bhopal, Bhubaneshwar and Mysore) found most children to be deficient in concepts and skills related to readiness for reading, writing and mathematics.[36]

A supportive environment – home and community:

With more children surviving into school age and being motivated to come to school, most tend to be first generation learners. But is the

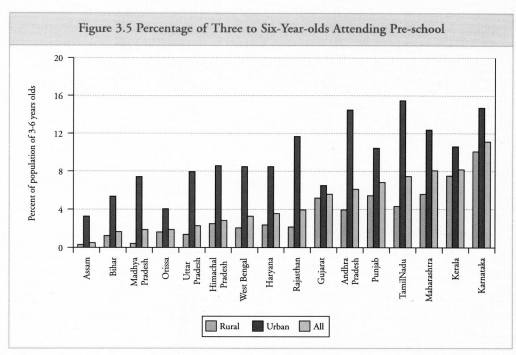

Figure 3.5 Percentage of Three to Six-Year-olds Attending Pre-school

Source: Indicus Analytics 2003 – Analysis of NSS 55th Round: 1999-2000

---

[35] NCERT 1998.

[36] Upadhyay et al 1999.

child's environment supportive of school learning? Surveys across the country show that parents are interested in the education and development of their children. But evidently there is little information in the larger community. The new generation of parents, in particular, often does not have access to extended family support systems when it comes to the developmental needs of the child at different sub-stages. The parents are losing some of the traditional childcare practices – such as massage, breastfeeding and infant games – that created spontaneous, family-level interaction between parent and child. Across the country, and specifically in economically disadvantaged families or nuclear families, parents are losing even the significance of responsive parenting and childcare, including the value of play for the child. As a result, more parents are ill informed and push children at an early age toward "miseducation", with its distorted emphasis on formal teaching of the 3R's (reading, writing and arithmetic), which often leads to what is referred to as a "damaged disposition towards learning" So the home environment is, all too often, not supportive of school learning that is really beneficial to the child.

The case studies also report that most children received little cognitive stimulation at home, and are left on their own to play and wander around. Few children accompany their older siblings to school since there is no specific provision for them. Amazingly, even at this young age, children are seen taking responsibilities for small tasks related to sibling care, household chores, or cattle care. This situation, coupled with nutritional deficiency and frequent illnesses, means an unpromising prognosis for these children – in terms of developing the necessary cognitive readiness for later schooling, and the probability of successfully completing primary schooling.

Sub-stage 4 (six to eight years):
Enrollment in primary school:

It is seen that enrollment in pre-school is far from satisfactory; but there is better news at the primary school level. According to NFHS-II data, 80 percent of all 6-7 year olds were enrolled in school by 1998-99, increasing from 64 percent in 1992-93. The gender gap has been reduced from 10 to 5 percent which is a significant achievement. There has been a substantial increase in the

Three to Six Years : Findings and Priorities for Action	
Findings	Priorities
High under-five mortality; high incidence of water-borne, diarrheal and communicable diseases.	Nutritional support, immunization, safe water, sanitation facilities and hygienic practices.
National average is only 15 percent enrolled in pre-school; lower in rural areas.	Operationalizing pre-school component at ground level, particularly in rural areas, and improving quality of ECE.
Inadequate parental support despite interest; overemphasis on formal education; inadequate community information.	Revival of useful traditional childcare practices; awareness regarding play-based learning.

enrollment of SC (from 57 to 76 percent) and Scheduled Tribe (ST) (47 to 67 percent) children during the period 1993 to 1999. So despite some variations by state and socioeconomic background, it is safe to say that getting children enrolled in schools is no longer a required critical input.

Regular attendance and retention:

However, the bad news is that the majority of children are "at risk" of dropping out of the system at this stage, with less than 60 percent ultimately completing primary education. Among primary school children, poor nutrition and health are frequent causes of poor enrollment, absenteeism and early dropout. Conditions like worm infestations, and deficiency of iodine and iron tend to be very common at this stage, and they affect the children's cognitive abilities and general well being, leading to lower levels of motivation and achievement. In terms of health status, children continue to demonstrate significant

levels of morbidity. And there is considerable direct and indirect evidence of higher morbidity among girls. These factors are also likely to lead to lower utilization of available educational services. When children's health and nutrition are poor, efforts to improve quality of teaching-learning are rendered ineffective as children are unable to take full advantage of the educational stimuli that schools offer. In this context, poor sanitation and the absence of a functional school health program continue to have a negative impact on the child's education.

Children also attend school with varying degrees of regularity, either because of poor health or because of work. In some places, children support their families by taking care of cattle. Children, particularly girls, also have to contribute to household work such as fetching fuel wood, fodder, or water and take care of younger siblings. They have to run errands and look after

The children reported that on most days, several of them (almost 10-15 percent) go to school without eating. This is particularly true of girls, given their burden of morning chores in the household. What impact does this short-term hunger have on their learning?

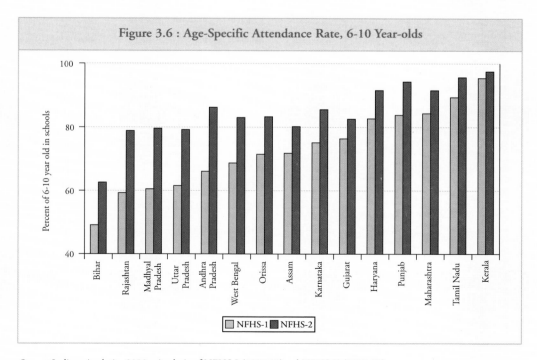

Figure 3.6 : Age-Specific Attendance Rate, 6-10 Year-olds

Source: Indicus Analytics 2003 - Analysis of NFHS I (1992-93)and NFHS II (1998-99)

sick family members. As such, these children are either late for school or miss it altogether. Given the large number of children dropping out of school during this sub-stage or not attending school regularly (see Figure 3.6), the main challenge is to keep children in school and promote their retention.

Support at home and in the community: Poverty does remain a major obstacle to schooling. So does the home environment – in terms of the large number of children, and the lack of education of the adult members, especially of women. The community's general biases also loom large in the child's health, nutrition and education chances. For example, the situation of the child is closely linked to the situation of women in the community. Remember Kamla the responsible dropout? Unfavorable cultural biases towards girls and women, along with their burden of household and sibling care responsibilities, often tend to keep the girl child out of school. Restraints on women's freedom, and unequal access to basic social services, also place young girls and women at a disadvantage. These "disadvantages" make themselves felt in many forms: for instance, in widespread anemia and malnutrition among adolescent girls. Later, in the case of pregnancy, this affects the newborn child, and the vicious cycle continues.

It is not just gender that affects the child's chances by excluding her or limiting her access to the health, nutrition and

Six to Eight Years: Findings and Priorities for Action	
Findings	Priorities
Significant increase in primary school enrollment rates.	**Promoting regular attendance and retention:** freeing girls from sibling care by expanding ECCE and crèches; setting up school health program; increasing teachers' accountability; sensitizing teachers to children's emotional needs; using IEC to promote awareness; discussion among parents and community on relevant quality education, nutritional and health support for school children, and overcoming gender/caste/class biases.
High rates of absenteeism.	
High dropout rate.	
Poor quality education: rigid, uninteresting and examination-driven curriculum and classroom practice; inadequate time on task; low teacher-pupil ratio; and long and inflexible school timings.	
Obstacles to regular schooling include poverty, work, caste, disabilities, poor health and nutrition inputs.	**Improving quality** by making texts and tasks more relevant and free of stereotypes; increasing time on task; improving teacher-pupil ratio; and involving community in defining and evaluating quality.
Inadequate support: teachers' biases, community biases and parental ambiguities.	
Sending children to school has become community norm in rural Andhra Pradesh and Karnataka.	**Extending community norm** of sending children to school.

education she needs but caste and poverty also continue to exclude children from the mainstream and limit their participation and learning in school. And most schools are unable to cope with children with even mild physical and mental disabilities. This brings us to the next question: how well do the schools – and the teachers - fulfill their share of responsibility for the child's holistic development?

The schools and teachers, and the issue of quality:

It is not just the community and home environment that makes children drop out, or stay away from school but it is also the schools and the teachers that cause this. About 47 percent of those children who drop out of schools leave because they are unable to cope with failure or the teacher's biases, or because they are not interested in what is being taught.[37] Many children express a desire for teachers who will not "shout" at them, humiliate them or make them scared.[38] This is the verdict of far too many primary school children and their parents. Their verdict eloquently describes the quality of schooling they are getting - the case studies indicate that the school structure and curriculum generally fail to respond to different social backgrounds and entry levels. The curriculum tends to be rigid, with high and uniform expectations for the early grades. Equally discouraging is the tendency of the curriculum to be un-interesting and information-loaded; of school timings to be long and inflexible; and of classroom practice to be assessment-driven, emphasizing rote learning at the cost of higher mental abilities.

The nature of the task is all too often dull and monotonous; and the time on task frequently inadequate.[39] The low motivation level of teachers compounds the problem for most children.

The low teacher-pupil ratio and the teacher's lack of accountability were observed to be matters of concern and so was the need for relevant reading material in schools and homes. Community members expressed a general ambivalence about the value and quality of education. They were confused about whether education can actually change their lives and enhance their self-esteem. They described their dilemma by citing the reality that the lives of their role models have not changed despite formal education; and by observing that many children who attended school for 4-5 years were unable to read or write fluently. But despite this ambiguity, discussions in rural Andhra Pradesh and Karnataka revealed that sending children to school has become the community norm. This is yet to emerge fully in Uttar Pradesh.

Sub-stage 5 (eight to eleven plus years):

By the eighth year, the child is, or should be, getting closer to completing primary school. Obviously, the child has to continue to attend school as attendance is critical, just as the quality of schooling is. The child needs to be taught basic skills. Equally important, the child needs to develop curiosity and a desire for lifelong learning.

We have earlier indicated that successfully completing primary school is a

---

[37] National Sample Survey Organization (NSSO) data (52nd round).

[38] Ramachandran et al 2003.

[39] Kaul et al 2003.

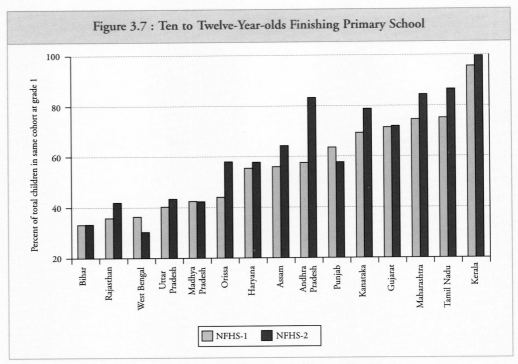

Figure 3.7 : Ten to Twelve-Year-olds Finishing Primary School

Source: Indicus Analytics 2003 – Analysis of NFHS I (1992-93) and NFHS II (1998-99)

"milestone-measure" of the child's holistic development. It is also a measure of how well existing programs and services are working for the child's development. Considering completion status of primary education as an indicator of the impact of the existing programs and services, the conclusions are not encouraging:

- The data indicates that though enrollment rates had risen significantly, from 73 percent in 1993-94 to 83 percent in 1998-99, the completion rates had risen only by 5 percent.

- Retention and completion rates remain major issues, with almost 40 percent (ranging from almost nil to 65 percent) of enrolled children dropping out of school before completing primary education (Fig. 3.7). This also results in wasteful and inefficient use of public resources.

- In addition, there was the question of whether most children would be able to attend school without interruption - either because of ill health, or because the children may need to work, or because the school did not motivate children or their parents to ensure regular attendance.

- And among those who do survive the primary education cycle, achievement levels remain deplorably low. Given the non-detention policy of several states, children who have the required attendance are promoted to the next grade regardless of learning achievement with the consequence that learning deficit is carried on to next grade. The health and nutrition status of children is also, as we have seen, far from satisfactory. Thus, while the transition rates from the primary stage to the upper primary stage are very high, a serious issue remains to be addressed – helping children survive the lower primary grades and emerge, having completed the cycle, as well educated and healthy children.

Across the Stages: The Burden of being Different

To look at the specific needs of the whole child at every stage and sub-stage, it is necessary to understand the current status of Indian children not only in the aggregate, but also as a part of different groups. Does being a rural child make a difference for example? Or being poorer than others, or being a girl, or of a lower caste, or from a particular state in India? And do all these factors add to each other's effect on the child?

The rural Indian child's chances at development continue to lag behind those of her urban counterpart. Substantial economic disparities operate across location (rural/urban), caste and gender for children of all ages. A comparison of the poorest rural quintile with the richest urban quintile indicates the extent of disparity between the extremes - the most privileged at one end of the spectrum, and

the most disadvantaged at the other. Poverty in the urban context also requires specific mention, given the disadvantages suffered by the children of urban slums. Using all outcome indicators for which quantitative date was available, Table 3.2 clearly identifies the target group requiring interventions.

As was discussed in the earlier stages of development, the girl child tends to have unequal chances at holistic development. These gender-based disparities are generally more apparent among older children, and are particularly evident when it comes to completing primary school. And the girl child's disadvantages are sharpened if she lives in a rural area and belongs to the lower income quintiles.

What does it mean to be an Indian child from a SC or tribe? Sadly, it means the child is marked by disadvantages early in life (see Figure 3.8). Belonging to an ST-household, for example, substantially reduces the likelihood of full immunization of the one-year-old child. Being an SC child means doing a little better than the

Eight to Eleven Years: Findings and Priorities for Action	
Findings	Priorities
Enrollment rates have risen by 16 percent, but completion rates have risen only by 5 percent. Irregular attendance due to poor health, work, lack of motivation. Low achievement levels among those who complete primary school.	**Promoting regular attendance and retention** by freeing girls from sibling care, school health program, teacher training and increasing teacher's accountability, promoting information/ awareness/ discussion among parents and community on relevant quality education, nutritional and health support for school children, and gender/caste/class biases. **Quality of alternative schooling** and issue of equity with formal education.

Table 3.2 : Economic Disparities in Outcome Indicators		
Indicator	Rural: lowest economic quintile	Urban: highest economic quintile
Proportion of underweight mothers	47.23	8.57
Proportion of anemic mothers	31.42	26.17
Proportion of mothers who took iron folic acid tablets	35.91	89.59
Proportion of infants not born underweight	51.47	66.87
Proportion of children (one month to 3 years) not underweight	78.87	92.63
Proportion of one-year olds immunized	28.63	81
Proportion of two-year olds given Vitamin A supplements	22.83	52.84
Proportion of 6-7 year olds enrolled in school	64.1	98.15
Proportion of 8-10 year olds enrolled in school	69.7	98.6
Proportion of 10-12 year olds completed primary school	21.62	67.15

Source: Indicus Analytics 2003 – Analysis of NFHS II (1998-99

ST child as far as pre-school and regular school enrollment are concerned; but it still means less of a chance of having received Vitamin-A supplementation than children who are not SC or ST. Whatever the differences between belonging to an SC or an ST, the child from either group is less likely to complete school than a child from the "general" category.

Which state a child lives in also makes a difference. And what is particularly

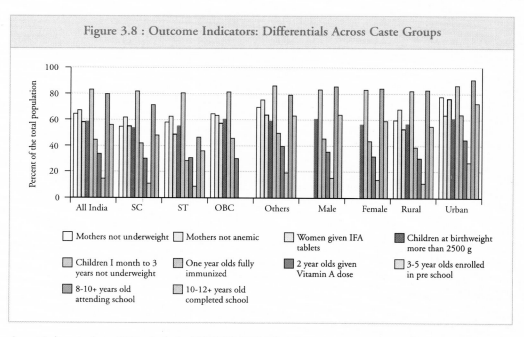

Figure 3.8 : Outcome Indicators: Differentials Across Caste Groups

Source: Indicus Analytics 2003 – Analysis of NFHS II (1998-99)

worrying is that it is precisely those states with poorer indicators that also show larger disparities for all aspects – gender, location, caste and economic status. The disparities begin at the neonatal stage of the child's development – over half the mothers surveyed in states such as Bihar, Rajasthan and Uttar Pradesh were anemic; at the other end of the scale were states such as Kerala and Tamil Nadu (see Figure 3.1). In general, children living in the southern and western states are more likely to be born to healthy mothers, have adequate birth weights, and, as they grow, receive immunization and Vitamin-A supplementation. They are also more likely to be enrolled in pre-school and school. Most of all, they are more likely to complete primary school - a proxy indicator for improved life chances.

Child Labor:

One important aspect of the burden of being different is that poverty compels many Indian children to work on a regular or continuous basis to support themselves or help support their families. The National Policy on Child Labor was adopted in 1987 to deal with such situations. The Policy encouraged voluntary organizations to take up activities such as non-formal education (NFE), vocational training, provision of healthcare, supplementary nutrition and education for working children. The three main ingredients of this policy are:

Different Children, Different Chances: A Summary of Findings

Rural/urban: Noticeable differences in proportion of underweight mothers and those who took IFA tablets, less likelihood of rural children enrolling in pre-school and completing primary school.

Income: Poor children have lower chances across location, gender, and caste. This includes children from urban slums.

SC: Lower chances than non-SC/ST children for all measures including pre-school and regular school enrollment, and Vitamin-A supplementation.

ST: Even lower chances than SC, including chances of full immunization at age one; disparities increase with age.

Gender: Disparities increase as girls grow older, and affect completion and repetition rates.

State: Children from northern and eastern states less likely to have healthy mothers, adequate birth weights, immunization, Vitamin-A supplementation, enrollment in pre-school, primary school, and completion.

Data analysis of the various groups, and disparities within and among groups, shows that across sectors and the stages of development of the child, children from the disadvantaged groups in the population are moderately to substantially worse off than the privileged groups for the outcome levels achieved by children. The specific aspects that this analysis of disparity highlights could be critical for decision-making at the policy level. That states with poorer indicators also have larger disparities with respect to gender, location, caste and economic status -which is of even more concern to the policymaker.

"I bring in the firewood, get water, clean the house, cook and wash the vessels. I don't mind doing these things, but when I am tired, it's all too much."[41] The child's words express the increasing demands on the girl child as she gets older - to take care of siblings, get water, fuel wood and fodder, and sometimes, take care of the entire household - all demands that drain the time and energy that could be devoted to school. In one case study, children said that when they have work at home, they stop going to school; this is particularly true of the two harvest seasons (April/May and October/November). Under the DPEP and current *SSA*, a concerted effort is under way to bring working children to school by providing various models of "bridge programs." But whether the children escape work by coming to school or double their burden of work remains debatable. Overall, the current situation is that despite numerous schemes and programs, a significant number of Indian children are still out of school. Thus the need of the hour is social consensus on the primacy of primary education. The Total Literacy Campaign, for instance, has led to a "tremendous enhancement of demand for primary education and enrollment of children in primary schools" in many literacy campaign districts.

(i) a legislative action plan for strict enforcement of the legal provisions; (ii) general development programs for child labor where possible; and (iii) a project-based action plan in areas where child labor is highly concentrated. But the reality of child labor continues. The 1991 Census indicates that as many as 11.28 million Indian children are laborers.[40] Of these, the most vulnerable are girls, and those children who are "bonded laborers."

Though the additional work the child does at home cannot be called "child labor," this too impedes their regular attendance in school, their levels of learning, and their successful completion of primary school. In a child's words:

What are the factors responsible for the unsatisfactory situation regarding the child's completion of primary school?

- Child labor is usually attributed as the primary reason for keeping children out of school.

---

[40] DWCD, MHRD, GOI 2001j.

[41] Ramachandran et al 2003.

- Parental commitment to female education may still be weak in certain areas. Cultural factors and social institutions also play an important role in molding parental attitudes to female education.

- Being favorably disposed to the education of children is one thing but surmounting barriers of accessibility, affordability and quality, and translating disposition into action is quite another.

The proportion of parents who considered it important for their children to be educated was high for both boys and girls, even in the more backward states.[42] This perception, as well as the incentive of the midday meal, motivated more parents to enroll their children in school. But a large number of parents were not equally motivated to ensure regular attendance or retention of their children in school. For this they cited poor quality of education as the main reason. The problem of poor quality also hindered the formation of a social norm of sending children to school, so that the parents' ambivalence was only further reinforced.[43]

A Summary of Conclusions: How has the Indian Child been doing over the Past Decade?

The responses to the question about the Indian child over the last decade are mixed. On the one hand, there have been positive changes. For instance,

- Efforts such as the RCH program's awareness campaigns have helped

provide free iron folic acid tablets to pregnant women and have had some impact. There has also been a significant increase in the number of children who get Vitamin A supplementation; and this improvement is largely explained by a 9 percent increase for SC children, and a 13 percent increase for ST children.

- The proportion of children fully immunized has increased from 37 percent in 1993-94 to 45 percent in 1998-99.

- Over the last 15 years, the enrollment of 3-5 year-old children has improved from 5.3 percent in 1986-87 to 14.5 percent in 1999-2000. The enrollment of 6-7 year olds has also increased substantially over the decade, from 64 percent in 1992-93 to 80 percent in 1998-99. Again, for 8-10 year olds, enrollment rates have risen from 73 percent in 1993-94 to 83 percent in 1998-99. Completion rates also increased, though by the much lower figure of 5 percent.

- The gender gap has also reduced from 10 to 5 percent, and SC and ST enrollment has increased from 57 to 76 percent and from 47 to 67 percent respectively between 1993 and 1999. The divergence among quintiles has also been falling over the decade.[44]

But despite these relatively positive changes, the overall impact has not been as powerful as that inecessary to meet the challenge of the current situation. And the overall impact does not quite match with

---

[42] PROBE Survey findings, 1999.

[43] Ramachandran et al 2003.

[44] Indicus Analytics 2003.

what was put in - whether in terms of plan and project efforts, or in terms of spending. Just a few instances illustrate this conclusion:

- The proportion of infants weighing less than the standard 2500 gms at birth has actually increased, though the average birth weight of the child has remained about the same at about 2800 gms over the decade. This worrying sign may be related to feeding down practices.

- The improved figure of children fully immunized is still a poor indicator. Besides, the increase is for the most part explained by improvement in figures for urban children and children from upper castes. ST children continue to lag behind.

- Despite the improvement in enrollment of 3-5 year-old children, the overall number continues to be very low. This is particularly significant, considering how critical cognitive development at this age is for future success in remaining in school as well as learning well.

Child Development Index:

It is amply clear that the current status of children is far from satisfactory as far as separate indicators are concerned. Going beyond this finding, this research also attempts to see the relative consistency across indicators by consolidating these as a Child Development Index (CDI). Such an index is of value for an overall assessment of the Indian child's current status and as a tool for policy planning. (See Box 3.2 for the methodology of arriving at CDI.)

The CDI in Figure 3.9 has been calculated for two time periods, for NFHS-I (1993) and NFHS-II (1999); and this figure illustrates a definite improvement in child development in all states. However, the level of improvement is better for those states that are already higher on the CDI. The analysis of the indicators for child development also illustrates a significant positive relationship: the states performing poorly on one indicator perform poorly on most of the other indicators. And the indicators are evidently interdependent as well – thus reinforcing the need for a multi-sectoral, convergent approach. Though all the states have improved their

---

Box 3.2 : Arriving at CDI

The CDI is proposed as a measurement of average achievements in a country with regard to basic dimensions of child development including: (i) Infant Survival Rate (ISR- the direct opposite of IMR); (ii) One year old children with full immunization (FI); (iii) School enrollment (NER); (iv) School Primary Completion rate (PCR). From these, CDI was calculated giving equal weightage to all the indicators. That is,

$CDI_j = 1/4 * \sum_j (X_i)$; Where CDI_j is for the jth state, i indicating the indicators used such as the ISR, FI, NER and the PCR. So,

Child Development Index (CDI) = (ISR*0.25) + (FI*0.25) + (NER * 0.25) + (PCR*0.25)

Note: CDI was calculated using the same methodology as was used by the Planning Commission, GOI (2002) for calculating its HDI. See the Technical Appendix of the Planning Commission, GOI (2002) National Human Development Report for details.

performance between 1993 and 1999, the all-India average (69.13) is still a matter of concern – particularly when compared to the more acceptable range demonstrated by states like Himachal Pradesh (91) and Kerala (92). It is clear that the national average has been pulled down by the lower levels of improvement of states such as Bihar, Rajasthan, Uttar Pradesh, Assam and West Bengal which too depict a wide range from 49 in Bihar to 64 in Assam. These states, in fact, show a cumulative pattern of disadvantage across the indicators. Not only are they unable to take advantage of existing schemes which they need the most, but also their capacity for utilization of interventions is limited possibly due to weaker governance. Such a syndrome makes it imperative to target these states more specifically if the national average on the CDI is to be improved and the MDG achieved.

Factors that affect going to school and staying there:

How does the overall impact of the findings, both positive and negative, affect the child's going to school? And more important in the current situation, affect regularly attending and completing primary school?

Let getting to and staying in school be visualized as a game, somewhat like snakes and ladders. The board (see Figure 3.10) would depict the child's life circumstances, and each row is a different layer of life circumstances, starting with the most immediate to the most distant. Perhaps one can imagine the snakes as the circumstances in each layer that will move the child backward and bring her home. The ladders are the circumstances that help the child to progress, either to the next layer, or to school against all odds. The length of the

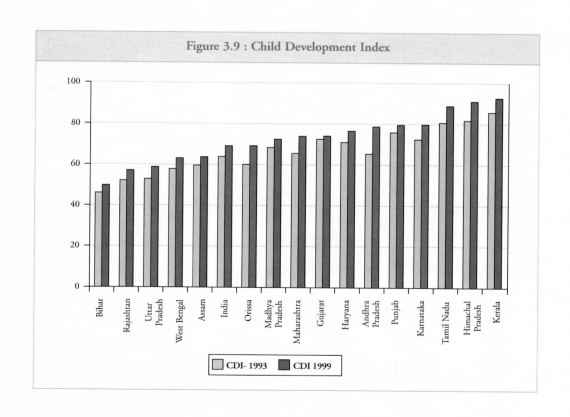

Figure 3.9 : Child Development Index

CDI- 1993   CDI 1999

snake or the ladder is determined by the relative strength of that factor.[45]

Tying up the qualitative findings – the trends indicated by this board of factors that affect getting to school and staying there – with the quantitative findings discussed earlier, it is concluded that Indian children are still a long way off from the optimal life chances they need for their development. It is this mixed, real picture, with its variations among frames, which must be addressed by policymakers when they plan and implement projects and schemes for the Indian child.

---

[45] The list is open, and more factors can be added. The figure is from Ramachandran et al 2003.

Figure 3.10 : Snakes and Ladders: Factors that Affect going to School and Staying there				
Snakes: + Mild ++ Strong +++ Very strong ++++ Exceptionally strong				
Snakes	Mild	Strong	Very strong	Exceptionally strong
Being a girl		++		
Being the oldest child			+++	
Having no sisters		++		
Being one of many children		++		
Having a parent with disability		++		
Having a mother who goes to work for long hours			+++	
Having an uncaring mother			+++	
Having parent/s dependent on alcohol			+++	
Having a brother or sister with a disability (for girls)		++		
Going to a school that is too close (the children reportedly run home)	+			
Having a punitive teacher who yells at and denigrates children of the poor		++		
Being from a lower caste, poor family		++		
Erratic participation in school due to work or social visits			+++	
Being sick or disabled			+++	
Having local youth or adults in community who have not benefited in terms of employment or income after schooling			+++	
Drought		++		
Hunger	+			
Ladders: + Mild ++ Strong +++ Very strong ++++ Exceptionally strong				
Snakes	Mild	Strong	Very strong	Exceptionally strong
Having a mother who values education for the child			+++	
Having a mother who is concerned about her child's welfare			+++	
Being a boy		++		
Having other adults living with the family who can care for younger children and supervise the home			+++	
Having fewer siblings, but not being just one or two			+++	
Having been breast-fed+				
Being in good health	++			
Having teachers who are affectionate, or at least don't yell and beat up children				++++
Having parents or even one adult in the family who believes in the benefit of schooling			+++	
Having some local success stories of progress after attending school			+++	

Existing Interventions
ARE THEY REACHING
THE CHILD?

Existing Interventions
Are they Reaching the Child?

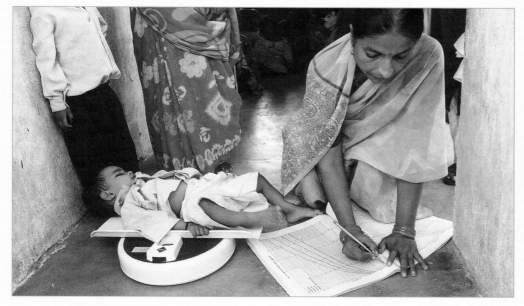

A child development policy has certain universal goals: "giving economically disadvantaged children the same chance to develop as their more fortunate peers, and addressing children's total needs by providing — where finances permit — an integrated package of services in healthcare, nutrition, and psychosocial stimulation."

Young 1996

Policies for the Child: An Overview[46]

We have seen that the Indian child's current situation demands major inputs — especially to reach the poorest and most socially excluded of children; to see to not some, but all aspects of their lives in totality; and most of all, to sustain this process of reaching out. Reaching out to the child means two very closely connected parts of a package of interventions: planning for the child's development; and effectively implementing the resulting programs and schemes that have been designed to put plans into action.

The root of the planning exercise is in the official commitment to children — beginning with the constitutional provision for the protection, development and welfare of children.[47]

The initial plans:

Against this background of commitment to the cause of the Indian child, the Government of India has, over a period of time, initiated several measures to ensure the survival, protection and development of children. This is reflected in India's Five-Year Plans,[48] which have launched

---

[46] This chapter is based on Devendra B. Gupta, 2003a, "Study of the Existing Policies & Related Provisions/Schemes for Promoting the Developmental & Educational Needs of Children in the Age Group Prenatal-11 Years." The study was undertaken for this Report.

[47] The Constitution of India, 1950. See Basu 1994.

[48] The various plan periods are as follows: First (1951-56); Second (1956-61); Third (1961-66); Fourth (1969-74); Fifth (1974-79); Sixth (1980-85); Seventh (1985-90); Eighth (1992-97); Ninth (1997-2002); and Tenth (2002-07). The periods 1966-69 and 1990-92 were covered by Annual Plans.

several schemes and programs to provide health, nutrition and education services. Indeed, plans for child development have been within the main frame of India's planning process from the very first Five-Year Plan (1951-56). In the initial years of planning, the main responsibility for developing childcare services was with voluntary organizations, whose efforts were assisted by the Central Social Welfare Board. But based on numerous studies which found acute malnutrition among school-going children, the First Five-Year Plan proposed a feeding program in addition to setting up public health departments that would take care of the needs of infants, children and mothers. With these initial interventions – disease control programs, more coverage, and better healthcare — India gained in human development achievements over the years.[49] But against these positive changes, the persisting problems stood out more sharply: high morbidity for instance, due to communicable diseases and nutrition-related diseases. It was in such a context that reviews and assessments of plans suggested that integration with other development sectors and their services was necessary for the holistic development of the child (see Box 4.1).

As a result, the succeeding Plans linked child development services with different sectors dealt with in each Plan, such as health, nutrition, family welfare, and education. Family planning services were integrated with maternal and child health (MCH) services, and nutrition programs extended to pregnant women and lactating mothers, and children up to the age of six. The MMS under the Applied Nutrition Program was introduced in schools and balwadis for pre-school children, paving the way for a subsequent integrated framework, as in the ICDS. Over the same plan periods, the need for expanding access to education was also addressed. After an initial period of emphasis on investment in higher and technical education, a new phase began with the 1968 Policy on Education, which emphasized programs that gave equal educational opportunities to both boys and girls and all social groups. In addition NFE[50] was introduced to cover the groups not reached by the regular system.

Box 4.1 : Why Choose an Integrated Approach?

Because a successful program of child development should:

- Exploit the complementary dimensions among the different aspects of health, nutrition, education and sanitation.

- Build strengths in delivery mechanisms of education, health and nutrition across the different stages of a child's development.

- Strengthen the delivery mechanism by involving active participation of the family and community.

---

[49] Life expectancy rose dramatically: from a mere 32 years in 1947, it went up to 61.1 years in 1991-96, with female life expectancy higher than the male. The decline in crude death ratio (CDR) was equally dramatic, from 25.1 in 1951 to 9.0 in 1996. Gupta 2003a.

[50] NFE, now evolved into AS.

Changing emphases – the Fifth Five-Year Plan:

The gradually shifting emphasis from child welfare to child development became more clearly articulated during the Fifth Five-Year Plan period (1974-79). Planning became inclined towards the integration and convergence of sectoral social inputs for the well being of infants, children up to the age of 6 years, and pregnant and lactating women. The government declared its formal position on child development by adopting the National Policy for Children (1974), which helped highlight various critical areas of child development and establish them as major areas of program planning. But most important of all was the milestone in the government's approach to child development: the conceptual move to integrate early services for children. Such integration was to cover a range of aspects, supplementary nutrition, immunization, healthcare including referral services, the nutrition education of mothers, pre-schooling, family planning, and the provision of safe drinking water. In keeping with this idea of integration, the Integrated Child Development Services (ICDS) was launched in 1975 to offer a package of services to children from the prenatal stage to the age of six, and to pregnant women and nursing mothers. The ICDS was to adopt a lifecycle approach, and cover the main components of holistic and sustainable child development — health, nutrition, and education. Its package of essential services was to be provided concurrently to make for a synergistic and holistic effect. As far as education was concerned, the goal of free and compulsory education for children up to the age of 14 years, which was to have

been achieved by 1960 according to the Indian constitution, remained (and has continued to remain) elusive, with the target date for its achievement being shifted again and again.

Consolidating and expanding programs – The Sixth, Seventh and Eighth Plans:

The Sixth (1980-85), Seventh (1985-90), and Eighth (1992-97) Five-Year Plans consolidated and expanded earlier programs. The family welfare program was linked with MCH and nutritional services; a National Health Policy was adopted (1983); and, in addition to the ICDS, ECE centers assisted to enable pre-school education. Since the late eighties, the family welfare program has evolved further, to a focus on the health needs of women in the reproductive age group — including the provision of contraceptives, and to a focus on the health needs of children below the age of five. The Universal Immunization Program (UIP), aimed at reducing mortality and morbidity among infants and younger children due to VPDs, was started in 1985-86. Oral Rehydration Therapy (ORT) was also initiated, given that diarrhea is a leading cause of death among children. Various other MCH programs were implemented during the Seventh Five-Year Plan, with convergent objectives. These were to improve the health of mothers and younger children by providing facilities to prevent and treat major disease conditions. Despite their beneficial impact, the discrete and separate identity of each of these programs led to less effective management, and to some extent, reduced outcomes. Hence, these programs were integrated under the Child Survival and Safe Motherhood (CSSM)

The conceptual move to integrate early services for children was a milestone in the government's approach to child development.

59

Program and implemented from 1992-93. The result has been a considerable improvement in indicators, though improvement has not been uniform in all the states.

In the area of education, since the 1968 policy was not translated into a detailed implementation plan that assigned specific responsibilities and accounted for financial and organizational support, a revised National Policy on Education was adopted in 1986 to meet the changing demands of India's economic, political and social goals. The policy goals were defined in broad and abstract terms, but Department of Education (DOE) followed this up with a comprehensive program of action detailing implementation strategies. To ensure that the state governments accepted the policy directives, the DOE took on most of the fiscal responsibility. This effectively opened the sector to external funding for basic education.

The 1986 National Policy on Education (NPE – 1986) was a policy landmark in the sense that for the first time, a policy on education recognized the need to invest in the very young child. It introduced the concept of ECCE to convey a holistic approach that would foster nutrition, health, and the psychosocial development of the child between conception and the age of six years. The approach included the erstwhile pre-school education component for 3-6 year olds, and "early psychosocial stimulation" for the under-threes, in addition to the health and nutrition components. The "early stimulation" subcomponent was to be implemented through parent education

and the use of the media; but it did not take off in any appreciable way. Also, while ECCE was defined as a holistic program, the programs for ECCE other than the ICDS remained largely unisectoral. And even in the ICDS, the synergies across the components, and along the continuum, were not adequately made use of, so that each component remained discrete. The other gain, thanks to the 1986 education policy, was the emphasis on the importance of play in ECCE. The policy cautioned against the use of formal methods to teach the three R's at the early stage of 3-6 years in the child's life. The Policy perceived ECCE as important not only as a foundation for lifelong development, but also as a program that would facilitate the participation of girls in schooling by providing alternative care to younger siblings, while providing support to working women.

The main focus of the Eighth Five-Year Plan (1992-97) was human development, with policies and programs for child survival and development receiving high priority. The National Nutrition Policy (NNP) was, as a result, adopted in 1993. Direct interventions for children included expanding the nutrition intervention net; empowering mothers with nutrition and health education; and ensuring better coverage of pregnant women. The experience gained from these initiatives, together with national and international consultations, culminated in an integrated and holistic program — the Reproductive Child Health (RCH) Program. Child health initiatives continued to be part of the overall MCH program framework. The earlier adoption of the NNP in 1993 also led to an expansion of the direct interventions net (ICDS, UIP and ORT). The Eighth Five-Year Plan also laid greater stress on children below the age of three. To this effect, two National Plans of Action were drawn up to provide guidelines for the "survival, protection and development" of children. One plan of action was for children in general; the other, adopted in 1992, was aimed exclusively at the girl child. Various indices were identified, and the target for achieving these was set as the year 2000.

At the same time, following the Revised National Policy on Education in 1992, the emphasis on universal primary education was reiterated, and expenditure on higher education began to show a downward trend. This period also saw the launching of several large-scale externally funded primary education projects, including the Bihar Education Project (BEP), the Uttar Pradesh Basic Education Project (UPBEP), the Lok Jumbish in Rajasthan, and DPEP. Subsequently, two major developments took place in the context of the commitment to eradicate illiteracy and raise the levels of schooling attainment among all marginalized social groups. First, the 73rd and 74th Constitutional Amendments were passed in 1992, providing for the decentralization of powers, and the assignment of responsibilities to a third tier of PRIs and urban local bodies. Since the basic function of democratic decentralization is to ensure that development planning responds to the regional and local needs of the population, primary education and primary health among the subjects included in the 11th and 12th schedule of the 73rd and 74th Amendments to the Constitution were transferred to the PRIs and urban local bodies.

The recent past – the Ninth Five-Year Plan:

The other major development was the recent clearance in 2002 of a Constitutional Amendment Act by the Parliament, which made elementary education for children between ages six and fourteen a fundamental and justiciable right. This development was expected to enhance allocations for elementary education at both the state and national levels. But unfortunately, this legislation did not cover children below 6 years. In response to the chorus of concern to this exclusion, the Government of India modified the earlier Article 45 in the Constitution to read "the state shall endeavor to provide ECCE for all children until they complete the age of 6 years," and included this modification as a constitutional provision.

The Tenth Five Year Plan emphasizes convergence and intersectoral coordination while pursuing a holistic approach to child development. But the mechanisms to operationalize this remain unclear. The challenge faced by the Tenth Plan is to innovate new designs, approaches, resources, and linkages rather than doing more of the same thing.

Thus, the Ninth Five-Year Plan (1997-2002), in continuity with its immediate predecessors, reaffirmed, that ECD was a priority for the country's human resource development. The Plan proposed a National Commission for Children to safeguard the constitutional and legal

The Tenth Five Year Plan emphasizes convergence and intersectoral coordination while pursuing a holistic approach to child development. But the mechanisms to operationalize this remain unclear. The challenge faced by the Tenth Plan is to innovate new designs, approaches, resources, and linkages rather than doing more of the same thing.

rights of children, and a National Charter for Children to delineate government commitments and resources for children. ICDS continued to be the "flagship intervention" for the overall development of children below the age of six, and was to be universalized by the end of 1995-96 by expanding its services all over the country.

Looking ahead – the Tenth Five-Year Plan:

The current Tenth Five-Year Plan (2002-07) reviews performance under the Ninth Five-Year Plan, and acknowledges that goals such as those related to MMR and IMR are not likely to be achieved.[51] As far as the universalization of ICDS is concerned, the review of the Ninth Five-Year Plan targets indicates that ICDS has not yet been universalized, though the total number of beneficiaries has recorded a rise.[52] The main problem has been, predictably perhaps, a resource crunch. The huge shortfall of about Rs 5000 million has not only affected the operationalization of sanctioned new blocks, but also hurt quality improvement initiatives.[53]

On the education front, the improved enrollment and attendance rates provide better news about Ninth Five-Year Plan targets as detailed in the previous chapter. School attendance rates rose sharply over the past six years; attendance levels of children in the 8-10+ age group were higher than those in the 6-7+ age group, indicating that the "survivors" had a higher motivation to continue and complete primary school.[54] The gap between boys' enrollment and that of girls had also narrowed.[55] But a great deal is still needed to be done on the critical front of quality of education, and the linked issue of retention of students in school.

In sum, the Tenth Five-Year Plan acknowledges the absence of a policy framework "that conceives and exploits inter and intrasectoral synergies between development processes directed at improving availability of drinking water, sanitation, public hygiene, access to elementary education, nutrition and poverty alleviation." It then takes a significant step forward with a well-articulated emphasis on convergence and intersectoral coordination in the course of pursuing a holistic approach to child development, as advocated in this report. But this progressive stance is mitigated by the fact that the mechanisms that will operationalize this convergence and intersectoral coordination remain unclear.

But the Tenth Five-Year Plan does spell out its intended strategies with reference to family welfare programs in general. These are to accelerate the pace of program implementation by streamlining infrastructure; by focusing on improved quality, coverage and efficiency of services

---

[51] Tenth Plan Working Group Report, GOI 2003a.

[52] Review of the Ninth Five-Year Plan, Working Group on Child Development for the Tenth Five-Year Plan, DWCD, GOI, 2003b.

[53] Ibid. The shortfall in actual allocation was Rs.2036.4 million in 1999-2000; Rs.1524.3 million in 2000-01; and Rs.1430.9 million in 2001-02.

[54] Indicus Analytics 2003.

[55] Annual Report, DOE, GOI, 2001k.

so that all the felt needs for family welfare are fully met; and by paying special attention to improving access to good quality services to the underserved population in urban slums and remote rural and tribal areas. In addition, the Tenth Five-Year Plan refers to operationalizing the Ninth Five-Year Plan strategy of preventing and managing anemia in pregnant women, and delivering the appropriate iron foliate treatment. It aims to work towards reliable MMR statistics on a sustainable basis, and to assess time trends and evolve programs to combat the major health problems of women. And it holds up as a goal the universal screening of pregnant women, using antenatal care to detect risk factors during pregnancy, and subsequently making referrals to the appropriate facility for treatment.

The Tenth Five-Year Plan has now taken on many intentions, goals and unfinished tasks from its immediate predecessor, the Ninth Five-Year Plan. The implementation of the ongoing Tenth Five-Year Plan will have to build on the strengths of its predecessors and learn from the lessons of past experiences. Most of all, rather than doing more of the same thing, the action plans will have to innovate new designs, approaches, resources, and linkages to deal with the urgent needs of the child it has inherited.

Acting on the Child's Behalf: A Review of some Major Programs
Major programs for the child – An overview.

From the point of conception, when the child's well being has to be seen in terms of maternal and child health, to the age of 11+ when the child should be successfully completing primary school, the major programs include those catering to the child before she goes to school; and those at the primary school level. The major programs for the pre-school stage consist of the RCH Program and the ICDS (see Table 4.1). The RCH, conceived to improve the health of mothers and the young child, has evolved into an integrated framework of various discrete programs. Services include health education to mothers on breast-feeding and immunization, Vitamin A supplementation, treatment of diarrhea and

Table 4.1 : Major Program Services for ECD, Prenatal-6 Years			
Programs include RCH ICDS	**Interventions** include maternal health, safe delivery, care of newborn, nutrition security including breastfeeding and complementary and responsive feeding, caregiver-child interaction, management of childhood illnesses, childcare practices, pre-school care and education, family and community support, environmental hygiene, safe water and sanitation, cultural attitudes and contexts.	**Components** include antenatal care, safe delivery, perinatal care, immunization, Vitamin A supplement, supplementary nutrition, and IEC strategy on health services, nutrition and health education, pre-school education, health and referral.	**Implementing agencies** include state governments, Department of Women and Child Development, and Ministry of Health and Family Welfare (MOHFW), GOI.

acute respiratory infection (ARI), and management of LBW babies. The RCH also has a significant component of IEC. The key worker at the grassroots level under this program is the ANM, who is supposed to work in coordination with the grassroots-level worker (AWW) of the ICDS.

Since its launch in 1975, the ICDS program has been the single largest nationwide program for promoting the holistic development of children up to the age of six. The ICDS was originally supposed to be universalized by 1996 but because of the shortage of funds, only 4,608 blocks could be operationalized by the end of the Ninth Five-Year Plan period out of a sanctioned total of 5,614 ICDS projects. Once universalized, the ICDS is expected to cover 54.3 million children and 10.9 million mothers. The World Bank-supported ICDS covers 1,953 projects, and through this support, additional inputs have been provided, such as the construction of project buildings, income generation activities for women and

mothers, experimentation of nutritional rehabilitation services, training in project management, and equipment.

The major programs for the primary school-going child include the *Sarva Shiksha Abhiyan (SSA)* and its predecessor, the District Primary Education Program (DPEP);[56] and the Midday Meal Scheme (MMS) (see Table 4.2). The DPEP is a centrally sponsored scheme (CSS) launched by the central government in partnership with state governments and external donor agencies. The objective is to expand the opportunities for poor and disadvantaged children to receive quality primary education. The *SSA*, the national program for universalizing elementary education, is a convergent umbrella under which previously discrete programs such as Operation Blackboard (OB) and Education Gurantee Scheme and Alternaive and Innovative Education (EGS & AIE) have been brought together. Moving beyond DPEP's coverage of Grades 1-5 in some project districts, the *SSA's* objective is universalizing education for all by 2015, and it extends its focus to Grade

Table 4.2 : Some Major Program Services at the Primary School Level, 6-11+ Years			
Programs include DPEP, *SSA*, MMS	**Interventions** include enrollment drives, community mobilization campaigns, establishing academic resource centers in-service teacher training, school and classroom construction, textbook and curriculum renewal, decentralized planning and monitoring, food adequacy, bringing "hard to reach" children into alternative schooling.	**Components** include primary education, noon meal, infrastructure, teachers including at least one female teacher, flexible timing for alternative schools.	**Implementing agencies** include voluntary agencies, and government at center, state, district and local levels.

[56] Hence the analysis of DPEP in this chapter applies to the SSA as well.

8, or children up to the age of 14. The SSA also has a special focus on the education of girls in areas that have been identified as having special needs as far as this provision is concerned. With its wider coverage and ambitious design, the SSA can, in a sense, be perceived as a response to the fundamental rights bill, which puts the onus on the government to provide elementary education to all children between the ages of 6 and 14.

The MMS, which had begun to provide nutrition support to school-going children, has grown into an extremely important input over the years. This has been further reinforced by the recent Supreme Court ruling (2002) regarding the provision of a hot cooked meal to be served to children in school. Given the fact that the existing system of formal primary education is not able to reach all Indian children, the scheme of NFE, was started in 1978-79, initially in the nine educationally laggard states. Later, it was extended to working children, and to urban slums, and hilly, desert, and tribal areas. The positive aspect of these alternative schooling centers is that they are able to reach marginalized groups and can expect more regular and accountable community-based teachers.

Before Getting to Primary School – ECD Programs:

We have seen that recent plans and policies have moved on to a lifecycle approach and a more holistic concept of child development. The crux of acting on the child's behalf lies, then, in the extent to which programs and services have been able to capture and exploit synergies across sectors, and along the development continuum, starting with the critical early years.

Reaching out to the newborn – prenatal to one month:

What are the priorities at this early stage to ensure a healthy and responsive newborn? The conceptual framework of this report has identified several important determinants: maternal health, a safe delivery, care of the newborn, breast-feeding and adequate nutrition, family and community support to the mother and the newborn, and a conducive package in the external environment – safe water, environmental hygiene and sanitation. In which case, the next question is whether existing programs and services for this critical early stage of the child's development actually address these determinants. At present, the major interventions are the ICDS and RCH programs, both partially supported by the World Bank. So, to what extent do these programs take on the preceding determinants?

Reproductive and Child Health (RCH):

During the Ninth Five-YearPlan period, efforts were made to improve the coverage content and quality of antenatal care through the RCH program, with the objective of a substantial reduction in maternal and perinatal morbidity. But the Tenth Five-Year Plan acknowledges that the maternal mortality rate (MMR) has not declined during the 1990s — more than 100,000 women still die every year because of pregnancy-related causes. The major causes of maternal mortality continue to be unsafe abortions, antepartum and postpartum hemorrhage, anemia, obstructed labor, hypertensive disorders, and postpartum sepsis. And all these causes are preventable: they could be overcome with improved access to safe abortion services, essential obstetric care, universal screening for detection of obstetric problems, referral and timely treatment of pregnancy complications, and institutional delivery and postnatal care. All these aspects are on the ground, but obviously they have not been adequately operationalized. For example, though anemia is a major cause of maternal mortality, screening for anemia was not included in antenatal care in any of the states.

The Ninth Five-Year Plan also emphasized the need to promote institutional deliveries in urban as well as rural areas. In districts where a majority of deliveries were taking place at home, all the *dais* (traditional birth attendants), were trained. Quantitative evidence does suggest some improvement in institutional delivery in states such as Tamil Nadu and Andhra Pradesh; but the majority of districts in many states do not report a satisfactory situation. This is supported by the qualitative data produced by the case studies.[57] On the one hand, neonatal mortality is high in states like Uttar Pradesh where most deliveries take place at home. On the other hand, NFHS-II data indicates that the decline in neonatal mortality in states such as Tamil Nadu and Andhra Pradesh has not been commensurate with their steep increase in institutional deliveries. The implication, clearly, is that the quality of intrapartum and neonatal care needs improvement in the context of institutional deliveries. This finding also raises a critical generic issue — the possibly linear relationship between the quality of service delivery and the community demand.

In the context of field data, we have seen the need for effective intersectoral interventions for appropriate health and nutrition education for adolescents, basic education, adequate health and nutrition interventions during pregnancy, and the advocacy of delay in the age of marriage. But though the RCH program has a significant IEC component for the health and nutrition education of pregnant women and mothers, it has not had an impact on the current situation – the intergenerational cycle of ill health and poverty. Among the reasons for this poor impact are the failure to "front-load" IEC into the program, not enough contextualization to the Indian scenario, and too much dependence on materials.

Overall, a review of the RCH program indicates that over the last thirty years, a very large infrastructure, based on uniform norms across the country, has been created for the delivery of health and family welfare services. But on evaluating this infrastructure in action, it is seen that it does not function as it should, primarily because of a mismatch between structure and desired functions, and because of the lack of any first line supervision mechanism to ensure accountability.[58] In the absence of an appropriate medical hierarchy with well-defined functions, accountability naturally could not be established. The program was also rendered less effective by inadequate

---

57 Ramachandran et al 2003.

58 Tenth Plan Working Group Report, GOI 2003a.

training and updating of technical knowledge, and a very poor communication component. And finally, RCH does not converge with the ICDS as well as it should.

The Integrated Child Development Services (ICDS):

It is noted that a shortage of funds has held up the universalization of this program. Also, despite the range of inputs into ICDS, a perennial issue across the states that has hampered effective implementation has been the lack of coordination between the *anganwadi* worker in the ICDS and auxiliary nurse-midwife in the RCH program.

Narrowing the focus down to just the ICDS, what has this ambitious program's impact been? Specifically, how effectively has it reached the child at this early sub-stage of her development? By design, the ICDS has focused on pregnant and lactating mothers, in terms of health and nutrition supplementation and education. It has also placed greater emphasis on 3-6 year olds rather than on the under-threes. Given this background of emphases, a midterm evaluation of ICDS in Andhra Pradesh and Orissa revealed both positive and negative findings. On the positive side, project interventions have been able to bring down the IMR to 62 and 93.6 per 1000 births respectively in the two states. The proportion of LBW babies has also come down to 20 and 23 percent in the states. But, on the less positive side, an ICDS document records that though there has been a rapid expansion of the service delivery network, the nutritional and health status of children below 6 years and pregnant/lactating mothers continues to be alarmingly poor after more than 20 years of

---

Box 4.2 : The Case of ICDS

Findings:
- Except for Kerala, there is a marked departure from standards for children's growth in all states.
- Overall, there is a high prevalence of malnutrition.
- Prevalence is higher in rural areas.
- Malnutrition begins very early in life and continues across the lifecycle.
- The direct causes include infant feeding practices, morbidity, and birth weight.

What can we do to prevent malnutrition now?
- Communication for behavioral change? Breastfeeding ? Complementary feeding 6-11 months.
- Convergence with RCH to reduce burden of illness ? immunization ? treatment ? hygiene.

What can we do about malnutrition in the longer term?
- Reduce poverty.
- Increase education coverage.
- Increase birth weight ? improve nutrition of adolescent girls ? improve nutrition of women during pregnancy ? increase age of women at first birth.

So what do we need to do about ICDS now?
- Increase coverage and attendance.
- Target under-threes, the poor, and adolescent girls.
- Communication for behavioral change (CBC).
- Converge with RCH.
  New strategies are required to make all this happen.

Source: Heywood 2003

program implementation. The document also says, "An evaluation of ICDS shows that nutrition and health education has been one of its most ignored services with most efforts and expenditures being focused on the provision of supplementary nutrition."[59] The case studies bear this out. Nutrition and health activities were found to be non-existent despite the presence of the AWW in the village and the monthly visits of the ANM.[60] Further probing elaborated on this finding: the ANM's monthly visit is, in many cases, limited to a specific area in the village, thereby missing out on reaching the more distant settlements inhabited by SC/ST groups.

There are, of course, differences in impact level among the states, largely due to differences in the overall governance environment. On the whole, for instance, the southern states show greater impact. But taking these differences into account, it is possible to conclude that implementation of ICDS continues to exhibit problem areas that undermine the project's holistic perspective (see Box 4.2). These problem areas include the over standardization of design and the corresponding lack of contextual relevance; unclear task definitions and unrealistic workload of the AWW; inadequate targeting of the poorest; underutilization of services, possibly linked to the quality of service delivery and the lack of accountability; and, as always, inadequate convergence with other sectors and departments.

Prenatal to One Month : Program Review	
RCH	ICDS
Large infrastructure in place.	Rapid expansion of service delivery network.
Inadequate operationalization: mismatch between structure and desired functions; poor quality antenatal care, often excluding screening for anemia; inadequate training and updating of technical knowledge.	Shortfall of funds, affecting coverage, expansion, quality improvements.
Poor accountability due to lack of appropriate medical hierarchy with well-defined functions.	Holistic perspective of program undermined: over standardization of design and lack of contextual relevance; inadequate targeting of the most needy; inadequate convergence with other sectors and departments.
Insufficient convergence with ICDS: lack of coordination between ANM and AWW	Underutilization, possibly because of quality of service delivery and lack of accountability; impact level linked with governance environment.
Poor communication component, weak on nutrition and health education of pregnant women.	Unclear task definitions and too much load on AWW.
Possible linear relationship between quality of service delivery and community demand.	Nutrition and health education neglected services.

---

[59] Communication for Behavior Change Action Plan – ICDS II, see GOI 1996b.

[60] Ramachandran et al 2003.

Reaching out to the confident and nutritionally secure toddler – One month to three years

At this stage, the critical factors include nutrition adequacy including breast-feeding and responsive and timely complementary feeding; the quality and consistency of interaction and relationship between the child and her caregiver, as well as early stimulation; full immunization and the management of diarrhea; adequate hygiene and health practices; and supportive cultural attitudes and traditions. This sub-stage of a child's life is often referred to as the growth faltering/promotion stage, since the child's brain development, language, cognitive and sensory motor development all occur at a rapid pace in these years. In fact, this stage is so critical for development that development lags in this period may often prove to be irreversible. If these years of the child's life are so important for lifelong development, the answer to the question of whether existing programs are meeting the needs of this sub-stage becomes very important for the Indian child's future.

RCH and ICDS:

A review of interventions for this critical stage, however, shows that existing interventions need to focus more effectively on children between one month and three years of age. This is particularly true for nutritional security — essential for the brain development that occurs during this development sub-stage. Despite the nationwide ICDS and RCH programs providing nutritional supplementation to pregnant women and children, the prevalence of anemia in women and in children (the latter as high as 74 percent)[61] shows that the current strategy of the anemia control program obviously has limitations. In apparent acknowledgement, there is a proposal to review the Anemia Control Program for

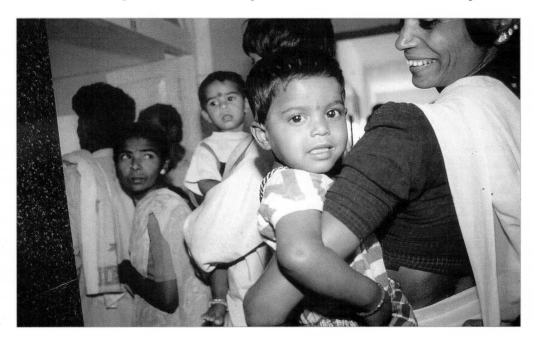

---

[61] NFHS-II, see IIPS 2000b.

Children and consider alternative delivery mechanisms[62]. And while the ICDS program has made some impact on severe malnutrition, moderate and mild malnutrition continue to be rampant – impairing the growth and cognitive development of children. A recent World Bank study[63] on five states showed that while there was a marginal difference in the prevalence of malnutrition between children attending and not attending anganwadis among the under-threes in Madhya Pradesh and Kerala, there was no such difference in Uttar Pradesh, Rajasthan and Maharashtra. This could be a factor for low attendance, linked to the distribution of food and its quality. Again, not much difference was detected in the consumption of solids or in complementary feeding between the children and families attending the anganwadis and those not attending. Whether it is the ICDS or the RCH, and whether it is children or pregnant women, the thrust of nutrition interventions is almost exclusively food provision. Since the related aspects of safe water, sanitation, good health services and hygiene have not been addressed in convergence with nutritional supplementation, direct investment on food has not yielded the desired returns in terms of reduced malnutrition.

For both the first and second sub-stages of development, early psychosocial stimulation becomes an important adjunct to nutrition. Responsive caring is not only an important determinant in promoting the child's overall growth and development, it also maximizes the impact of the accompanying nutritional intake. India already has a wealth of traditional early stimulation for the under-threes – whether it is infant games, or stories, or lullabies. A major need is for crèches for under 3-year age group to free the older girl siblings to attend school. These crèches should not merely be custodial but should also provide stimulating environment for the children.

The traditional childcare practices have been included in the ICDS training of the AWW so that they can make up a component in the mother's education program. But across the board, this effort seems to have been a non-starter, given that education and communication already comprise a weak program component. We have seen how the under-threes tend to be left in the care of older siblings, who in turn miss out on regular attendance of school, or on going to school altogether. Providing a crèche or a daycare facility to mothers with infants thus becomes an imperative, not just for the infant and the mother, but also for the infant's older siblings. Moreover, the ICDS-II has included income-generating programs for women to empower them and mitigate their poverty; in which case it becomes all the more necessary for their younger children to have crèches so that the women can participate in the programs meant for them. Some ICDS centers have in fact been extended to include crèches for the younger children. But these crèches are, for the most part, custodial in nature, as a result of which the

---

[62] The introduction of double fortified salt, and appropriate measures for de-worming is also being explored.

[63] World Bank 1998a.

child misses out on the early stimulation and psychosocial interaction that is seen to be important for development.

At this early stage of their lives, children are also vulnerable to significant childhood illnesses, and naturally this vulnerability is exacerbated by low weight, inadequate or faulty nutrition practices, and the threats of a poor external environment. Immunizing the child fully against Vaccine Preventable Diseases (VPDs) is, thus, an intrinsic part of any response to the needs of early child development. The Universal Immunization Program has had an impact on the number of cases of VPDs (see Table 4.3). However, achievement has fallen short of the 100 percent coverage expected by the year 2000 for all the six VPDs as per the National Health Policy of 1983 None of the states has achieved coverage levels of even 80 percent, coverage in Bihar, Uttar Pradesh and Rajasthan being quite low, and several states have reported a substantial decline in their routine immunization rates (Tenth Five-Year Plan, P.194).

One of the main reasons for the inability to achieve a 100 percent routine immunization has been the current focus on campaign mode programs in health and family welfare. An example is the case of polio, where campaign programs have constantly disrupted routine activities. The campaigns should, of course, continue so that polio eradication is not compromised.[64] But the lesson here is that the outreach for routine immunization too should be improved, perhaps by ensuring that the ANW visits all the targeted habitations.[65] And if the AWW were freed from the education of 3-6 year-old children, she would be in a better position to mobilize women and children for the ANM's visit.

There are several other reasons for the failure to achieve universal coverage, including the availability of vacancies at the ANM level; poor mobility; poor access; poor vaccine storage and poor distribution; and the lack of adequate supervision and monitoring.[66] Understandably, the

Table 4.3 : The Impact of Immunization, 1987-1999 (Number of Cases)			
Diseases	1987	1999	% Decline
Polio	28257	2817	84.7
Diphtheria	12952	2662	79.0
Pertussis	163786	20776	77.6
Neonatal tetanus (NNT)	11849	1767	62.1
Measles	247519	29135	84.2

Source: Working Group on Healthcare and Children for the Tenth Five-Year Plan, GOI 2001g.

[64] Though there has been a steep fall in polio cases (see Table 4.3), and the polio surveillance system has been strengthened, the current coverage of the PPI is around 90 percent.

[65] Habitation in the sense of different sections/ clusters of dwellings in a village.

[66] For an excellent exposition on reasons for poor coverage, refer to the Report of the Steering Committee on Family Welfare (Sept 2002), and the Report of the Working Group on Health Care and Children for the Tenth Five-Year Plan (June 2001), both from the Planning Commission, GOI. (GOI 2002a and GOI 2001g.)

government is seriously disturbed by the setback in the routine immunization program, and is taking the necessary steps to ensure that routine immunization is not disrupted. As far as vaccine storage is concerned, the government has established a cold chain system of transport and storage facilities to carry vaccines from the manufacturers to the beneficiaries while maintaining the recommended temperature. Most of this equipment, however, was supplied before 1988 and has outlived the normal lifespan of 10 years. The government is now replacing this equipment in a phased manner. A special emphasis on catch-up rounds and outreach services has also been proposed to improve coverage levels and wherever required, special campaigns would be undertaken for neonatal tetanus and measles. But other relevant factors remain. There has, for instance, been only a modest improvement in the availability of piped water or hand pumps to households across India: from about 68 percent, the figure has been raised to 78 percent between NFHS-I (1992-93) and NFHS-II (1998-99).

Reaching out to the confident and creative pre-schooler-three to six years:

In this sub-stage of development too, nutrition adequacy, and reduced incidence of intermittent diseases, continue to be areas that child development programs need to address. The quality of the home environment – adult-child interaction, the use of beneficial traditional childcare practices, and cultural and social attitudes and perceptions – are significant factors in the child's growth and development. At this point, the child also forms important habits related to health and hygiene, and inevitably, the health environment of the child remains relevant. As before, we have to examine to what extent current services meet this complex package of needs. Moreover, there is a major new requirement at this stage: access to a good quality ECE program. While survival and protection are among the first few building blocks of early child development, the major programs for the below-six cannot compromise on a component as important as pre-school education.

One Month to Three Years : Review of Programs	
RCH	ICDS
Current strategies of anemia control program inadequate	
Inadequate performance of UIP: 100 percent coverage not achieved; outreach services need improvement, several states report decline in routine immunization rates; disruption of routine activities by campaigns; poor availability of vaccines at ANM level, poor storage and distribution, poor mobility and access, inadequate supervision and monitoring.	Negligible difference in malnutrition prevalence and complementary feeding practices between children attending *anganwadis*, and those not attending.
	Income generation programs for women, but more and better crèches needed for their younger children; To enable their participation.
	Lack of psychosocial stimulation in existing crèches.
	AWWs trained in favorable traditional childcare practices (stories, lullabies), but this psychological component has not taken off.

The four major programs covering the sub-stage of 3 to 6 years are the ICDS, ECCE centers, pre-primary schools of state governments and municipalities, and daycare centers. The number of ECCE centers is dwindling because of the government decision to universalize ICDS and close other programs. *Balwadis* continue to run as pre-school centers, but they are being phased out, again because of the universalization of the ICDS schemes. And as far as daycare centers are concerned, though as many as 12,470 crèches have been set up to provide daycare for children up to the age of five, the program needs to be made more developmentally appropriate.

It is the ICDS program that is the main provider of ECCE. However, it needs to be acknowledged that ECCE is the first step in the education ladder. Despite the fact that the pre-school education component is one of the six services of the ICDS, in practice, ECCE is translated pretty much into nutrition centers, particularly in the northern states, as reflected in the case studies. Table 4.4 clearly brings out the task ahead, as less than 20 percent of the target group is covered by pre-school education.[67] The coverage needs to be substantially improved, considering the importance of pre-school education for the child's cognitive and social ability, as a foundation for all-round development, and as a factor that promotes enrollment and retention rates in primary schools. In fact, the actual number of children

Table 4.4 : Coverage under Various ECCE Schemes, 1996-97			
Program	Number of centers	Beneficiary coverage	Percentage of 3-6 year population covered
ICDS (pre-school education, age group 3-6 years) (2424 sanctioned projects)*	400,000	11,081,000	18.23
ECE	4365	153,000	2.7
Crèches and daycare centers, age group 0-5 years (estimated coverage on the basis of 25 children per crèche)	14,313	31,000	0.52
Balwadis (age group 3-6 years) (estimated coverage on the basis of 30 children per *Balwadi*)	5641	17,000	0.29
Pre-primary schools	38,533	194,000	0.33
Total		13,383,000	19.64

Source: DWCD, 1997; DOE, 1998 (See GOI 1997 and GOI 1998b)

* There are 4384 operational ICDS Projects with 578457 AWC and nearly 28 million beneficiaries. This includes 4.9 million expectant and nursing mothers, and 23.2 million children below the age of six belonging to disadvantaged groups. Of these, 15.5 million children (3-6 years) participate in center-based pre-school activities. Also ,there are 12470 crèche units covering about 0.3 million beneficiaries. (DWCD Annual Report 2000-01).

[67] This percentage may be somewhat higher if we also consider children attending schools run by NGOs and the private sector in the form of playgroups and kindergarten schools. These schools are largely confined to urban and semi-urban areas.

availing of pre-schooling under ICDS may have been lower if it were not for the supplementary nutrition component, particularly in the northern states.

The ICDS was introduced because it was recognized that larger economic and livelihood issues have a substantial impact on the nutritional status of poor children. But only a fixed or limited number of children have access to these ICDS services. Ironically, several of the children profiled in the case studies did not have access to the ICDS even though they were from poor families. The location, as well as the community or caste of the AWW was found to affect access.[68] Also, the quantity of supplements, and the regularity of their distribution, continue to present problems, especially in northern parts of Uttar Pradesh, and in Andhra Pradesh and Karnataka. Discussions with the women surveyed revealed that only a fixed number of children are admitted; many are turned away as the center could not accommodate more children.[69] But enrollment does not guarantee access to services. Some children in fact are merely enrolled; they are not necessarily attending or benefiting from the ICDS program.

The non-utilization of the *anganwadi* center service among children, particularly those of less than 3 years of age, may be the result of a perception that they are too young to be left alone. It could also be because the services being available only for half a day and alternative childcare arrangements are not available for the rest of the day. In addition, discrimination against children from lower castes or classes, the unhealthy and cramped environment in the *anganwadi*, and dissatisfaction with the food served at the *anganwadi* center are among the reasons cited for non-utilization.[70] This last reason becomes painfully relevant because many children come to the *anganwadi* without eating – or eating very little. The children observed in the case studies, for instance, were generally severely to moderately malnourished. As a result, any disruption in the supply of nutritional supplementation affects these children adversely.

Often, the *anganwadi* actually closes for weeks due to this disruption, providing confirmation that the centers function as nutrition centers only in some states. It has also been observed in the case studies that the provision of double ration to severely malnourished children is ineffective as these children are often unable to eat much at one go. There is, however, no evidence of any system in the *anganwadis* to identify the severely malnourished. Since state averages camouflage extreme inequalities, these observations, which are specifically for the poorest, may not be consistent. In sum, ECCE component is among the weakest of the six components of the ICDS package of services. The case studies, in fact, found this component almost non-existent, except for one *anganwadi* in one of the states, which

---

[68] For example, one AWW was averse to having SC children come to the anganwadi because her father-in-law objected to lower caste children coming there. Ramachandran et al 2003.

[69] All findings drawn from the case studies conducted in three states for this Report.

[70] Ranjan, Jayesh and K.A.V.R. Krishnamachari 1997.

was of good quality, largely due to individual interest.

ECCE as a policy issue:

The global knowledge now available through brain research, as well as Indian research on ECD, substantiate the conclusion that ECCE is an input of the utmost importance for lifelong learning and development. Moreover, studies across the world have shown ECCE to be a more cost-effective investment: it increases the returns to primary and secondary school investments through its significant contribution to the quality of children who enter primary schools, as well as through its contribution to the children's retention and their later learning. This in effect undermines the traditional argument that the state should give primary education the priority as

opposed to ECCE. In short, the need of the hour is the acknowledgement of ECCE as the first critical step of the education ladder. As children in the middle and upper classes can avail of privately provided ECCE, extending this to more needy children also becomes an issue of social equity. In this context, ECE cannot be seen as the sole responsibility of DWCD as it is at the present; the responsibility needs to be shared with DOE, with a separate budget created for the purpose.

Our analysis of findings indicates that several key issues of strategic significance remain to be addressed:

- In the light of the experience of the last thirty years, can the ICDS realistically take on full responsibility for ECCE of all children below the age of six?

Box 4.3 : How much can that One Worker do?

In the ICDS, just one worker with a helper has to:

- Provide a foundation for overall development (health, nutritional and psychosocial needs) of the child from 0-6 years. In practice this implies catering to the diverse needs of the multi-age group of 40 odd children, using an individualized approach; as well as catering to the needs of the 0-3 year olds by conducting parents'/mothers' orientation programs, home visits, and addressing the health and nutrition needs of pregnant and lactating mothers.

- Help 3-6 year olds to develop school readiness (pre-literacy and pre-mathematical skills and concepts) through the play-way method so as to retain them in school. In practice, this implies carrying out a well-planned curriculum with structured activities for the older children, particularly the 4-6 year olds, which, in nursery schools for example, is the sole responsibility of the teacher.

- Facilitate girls' participation in school by providing an alternative sibling care facility for younger siblings for the entire duration of the school hours, and including a crèche facility for the youngest sibling from 0-3 years of age. Children under the age of three are not expected to come to the *anganwadis*, but their care is an impediment to the girls' participation at this stage. Even more important, this is the critical stage in which to ensure that there is no growth faltering, chiefly by making sure the child is adequately nourished and free from illness. This should remain the responsibility of the ICDS, since it is habitation-based.

- Can one standardized model like the current ICDS – with ECCE as only one of its components, and with one honorary worker – cater to diverse needs and contexts? In addition to these diverse needs and contexts, the lone worker has to meet the needs of pregnant women, lactating mothers and adolescent girls; and any other responsibilities imposed by other departments. Most of all, the worker has to meet the many objectives of early ECD effectively (see Box 4.3).

The answers to questions about the future of ECD for the Indian child have to be based on the evidence provided by research on the current ICDS situation:

- While ICDS has had some impact, it is unrealistic to expect the current model to cater to all objectives and all contexts.

- Even more than the demand for the primary level, there is a growing community demand for ECD. But in spite of the attempt to universalize ICDS, many habitations remain unserved due to the ICDS norm of an *anganwadi* center per 1000 population, and 40 children to a center. With such an enrollment ceiling, even the "served" areas often see large numbers left out of the reach of service. This also raises the point about targeting. It has been said time and again that services need to reach the most disadvantaged. But to what extent is ICDS reaching this category of the poorest of the poor? The implication is that complementary ways of universalizing the provision of ECE must be considered.

- Given the DPEP experience and the states' own experience with pre-

primary centers, studies have consistently shown that when the school-based education sector model is compared with the habitation-based *anganwadi* model, each is found to have its comparative advantage in meeting the needs of the child's total development. Closer to the habitation and the children's homes, the *anganwadi* center model tends to be more appropriate for the younger child (0-3 years), and more likely to meet the child's holistic needs if the setup is enriched with play material, a more stimulating environment, and a crèche facility. But it has to be remembered that this model does not have the required conditions for an effective school readiness program for the 3-5 year olds despite recurrent training. As can be seen in Box 4.3, this is mainly because of the varied responsibilities of the AWW, who is now also required to shift her priority focus to the under-threes, the critical stage for the prevention of malnutrition. The school-based model, with its exclusive focus on the education component, is far more appropriate from the educational perspective. It also helps the child to form a bond with the school. Hence the need to review the present arrangement and look for more "out of the box" solutions.

Finally, irrespective of the model, and the large investments made in ICDS, is it realistic to expect ECCE to have a significant impact when its quality is as poor as indicated by the studies? Can a non-negotiable, minimum essential quality be defined in terms of

> ## Box 4.4 : Some Tried and Tested Models
>
> ◆ The ICDS-DPEP convergence model: 0-3/4 year olds get covered by ICDS; 4-5/6 year olds are relocated physically and programmatically to the school as a pre-primary class. (This was successfully tried out in Madhya Pradesh and Assam DPEP models.)
>
> ◆ Two-worker model in the ICDS design: one for the 0-3 year age group and the other for the 3-6 year age group.
>
> ◆ Integrated ECE model: 3-8 year olds are covered, using a specific play-based curriculum to cover ECE and Grades 1 and 2. The model can be operationalized by attaching ECE to existing AS under DPEP and SSA. Serving as feeder centers for primary schools, this model has several pedagogical advantages in preparing children for the primary grades. These include more conducive learning conditions for the younger child. This is true not only for the transition from home to school language and continuity from ECE, but also in its curriculum focus on learning the three R's by the time the child leaves school, so that she can move to a self-learning mode in the higher primary stage if necessary.
>
> ◆ Home-based model: This model, tried out by National Council for Educational Research and Training (NCERT) and NIPPCD, can be operationalized as one possibility under the *Mahila Samakhya* Scheme by using, for instance, women's groups

infrastructure, materials, program content and worker/teacher quality and work load, which together make up a specified norm for ECCE? The review of the current ICDS interventions almost inevitably calls for an examination of alternative possibilities in the guise of some tried and tested models (see Box 4.4)

Apropos the importance of ECE, it needs to be pointed out that the current thinking of the government, as revealed by the Working Group Report on the Tenth Five-Year Plan, is inclined toward promoting universal access to ECCE to all children below the age of six. However, the policy still locates the entire ECCE age group of 0-6 years with the ICDS Program, with the responsibility of the DOE rendered negligible. The national program for universalizing elementary education, the *SSA*, also dilutes the focus on this age group by treating what should be a universal provision as an innovation.

The Tenth Five-Year Plan proposals include a rather large package: strengthening linkages between the ECCE program and primary education by co-locating ECCE/ICDS centers with schools; synchronizing timings; training functionaries; extending timing of centers; paying extra honorarium to *AWWs* for extended work; providing play materials and kits; and improving quality aspects of pre-primary schooling. At the same time, the Plan also talks of a shift in priority to the nutritional needs of the under-threes. This unwieldy package of priorities and goals highlights the question that remains unanswered – how is the ICDS to bear more responsibility without new supportive inputs, in terms of modified designs, as well as human and financial resources?

Finally, in addition to examining alternative models to the current ICDS, there is also a need to examine one particular programmatic issue with regard to ECE. With the mushrooming of nursery schools over the years, a large section of early education is in the private sector. And these schools are run with no supervision – no system of accreditation to speak of. The consequence is that there is a great deal of "miseducation" in the name of early education: the curriculum is all too often a downward extension of the academic curriculum for Grades 1 and 2, instead of a developmentally appropriate curriculum. Not surprisingly, this phenomenon has had several adverse effects on the young child, all of which can have latent and cumulative effects on the child's overall development. Some system of supervision/regulation is called for, while, at the same time, incorporating a strong IEC component into provisions for early education to strengthen community monitoring.

Reaching out to School Entrants and Ensuring Successful Completion:
At the school level programs for primary school children:

The interventions at this stage need to build on what went before as the early childhood interventions, to consolidate and sustain the gains already made. In reality, the interventions at this stage have to cope with the deficits that have accumulated in the child's brief life, and get the child to school, give her primary education of reasonable quality, and keep her in school till she completes the primary stage – a period hopefully long enough to increase her ability and motivation for lifelong learning, and to increase her life choices. Indeed, this stage is subdivided into 6-8 years and 8-11 years in India, given the consistent findings across the public system that the majority of dropouts take place between the ages of six and eight years. There is

Three to Six Years : Review of Programs		
ECCE Centers	Balwadis	Daycare Centers
Dwindling numbers because of ICDS universalization.	Being phased out because of ICDS universalization.	Needs to be more developmentally appropriate.

ICDS: the main provider, but ECCE is one of its weakest components.

Coverage: less than one-fifth of target group.

Poor access: location, caste/community of AWW relevant factors.

Poor services: more nutrition centers than pre-school, especially in Northern states.

Underutilization/ non-utilization: weak infrastructure, lack of material, alternative daycare required for rest of day, poor quantity of nutritional supplement and regularity of distribution.

Unmotivated workers: inadequate incentives, unrealistic job charts, occasional mismatching between training and work situation.

Poor monitoring and lack of community ownership.

Overall: overburdened, cannot take on more responsibilities without new supportive inputs such as modified design and financial/ human resources. Needs strong IEC component, supervision of mushrooming private schools.

compelling evidence for a closer look at the needs and requirements of the sub-stage of 6-8 years, and the extent to which they are being met.

In talking of dropouts, one is talking about the poorest community, in which sending children to school is not a social norm that creates its own pressure on parents and children. Hence the situation outside the school draws the child away from school at this initial stage, whether the situation is poverty, or poverty in combination with household demands and the freedom from biases to go out of the house. How can the school assert its "holding power" on the child? The only way in which the school can counteract the "outside" pressures on these disadvantaged children is by ensuring a joyful, child-centered methodology, a kind and considerate teacher, and plenty of meaningful activity. In addition, of course, the child must learn the basic skills of reading, writing and arithmetic in this sub-stage, not only to prepare her better academically, but also to give the child self-confidence and self-esteem — the best motivators for further learning..

Access and coverage:

There is no doubt that a number of the measures taken have improved access to primary education. A number of primary schools (including those in smaller habitations) have been established and the number of teachers including female teachers has increased. There has been some improvement in infrastructure and other facilities, although a large number of primary/upper/middle schools still suffer from deficiencies such as multi-grade situations, which tell on the efficiency of teaching and learning. The most important achievement of existing interventions has been the increase in enrollment rates. There have also been perceptible signs of progress in school attendance among the younger age groups[71] and female school participation has increased among the 6-11 age group.[72] Even better, this narrowing gender gap reflects a major increase in the enrollment of girls in the educationally backward states. These positive trends appear largely to be the outcome of recent initiatives to bring marginalized children into the schooling system, notably in the context of the SSA or EFA program, DPEP, and the National Program of Nutritional Support to Primary Education, also known as MMS besides some state-specific government and NGO initiatives.

But despite these gains, on the whole, universal enrollment has not yet been achieved. An assessment of progress in DPEP I and II project outcomes and interventions[73] concludes that the net impact of the program on enrollment has been positive, though small. Despite substantial enrollment increases in some states, and the reduction of gender differences (to less than 10 percent) in most districts, social disparities have not been decreased in keeping with the target. This is particularly true in the case of ST children.

---

[71] According to NFHS-II, school attendance in these age groups is nearly 80 percent. See IIPS 2000b.

[72] From 5.4 million girls in 1950.51 to 49.8 million in 2000-2001 (EFA National Plan of Action 2003)

[73] A Review of Educational Progress and Reform in the DPEP (Phases I and II), World Bank 2003.

Health and nutritional support:

If positive trends in enrollment are to make an appreciable difference to the child's learning, the child's overall development has to be reinforced by health and nutrition support. If the child's health and nutritional inputs are not keeping pace with the physical and mental growth demands at the primary school stage, the results could be short-term hunger, degrees of malnutrition, chronic fatigue, or physical illness – all which not only affect learning levels, but also regular attendance in school. We have seen that the data indicates less than satisfactory attendance and retention; and that short-term hunger and its impact on learning is very much in the picture, particularly for girls. Most important for this student population vulnerable to short-term hunger and degrees of malnutrition, the MMS has been introduced to improve children's enrollment and attendance in primary schools, as well as their retention.

But the absence of a functional School Health Program in most states continues to be a factor in irregular attendance, dropout or low achievement levels for health reasons. The children's health problems in the case studies clearly showed their vulnerability at this age to diarrhea, skin diseases and regular bouts of fever, particularly during the change of season. With virtually no locally available facilities, children usually take some off-the-shelf medicines and rest at home till they recover.[74] The children also reported that when they have severe colds or body ache from carrying weights, or when they hurt themselves, they stop attending school. In this context, a School Health Program would not only have an impact on absenteeism, but also lead to the better learning and participation that comes with better health, while fostering better health and hygiene habits. Overall, the relation between health and education is too often perceived as a one-way street, and the critical and reciprocal link between education and health is ignored to the detriment of attendance in school, as well as educational attainment and achievement.[75]

Besides this shortfall in health and nutrition inputs, what kind of impact have existing programs made on the critical concern of retention? The assessment[76] is that though gender disparities were reduced in three quarters of districts, the goal of cohort dropout rate was achieved in very few districts. The assessment also concludes that the goal – less than 10 percent – was probably too ambitious in the first place.

Quality of education:

The issue of poor quality comes up time and again as a cause of irregular attendance, lack of retention and completion, and achievement levels. How have the existing programs fared with this most critical issue?

- Achievement levels: The assessment of both phases of DPEP program concludes that the target of 40 percent

---

[74] Ibid.

[75] Ibid.

[76] Ibid.

score in language and mathematics has been achieved in Grade 1 in most districts, but in less than five percent of districts for Grades 3-4. Only half to three quarters of project districts raised achievement levels by 25 percent over the baseline figure for Class 1, again because the target was probably too ambitious. Most districts have reduced gender disparities but have attained only limited success in reducing other social disparities, as in the case of SC and ST children.

- Teachers: Problem areas have included the worsening teacher-pupil ratio and the teachers' insufficient understanding of the children, particularly the needs of first-generation learners from disadvantaged sections. The Operation Blackboard Scheme (OB) and District Institute of Education and Training (DIET) have attempted to make a difference to this situation through training of teachers, but a review of their impact indicates operational problems. The OB scheme has experienced several problems in connection with the shortage of teachers, which has not increased in line with enrollment increase. While there was major recruitment of teachers in the nineties to convert single-teacher schools to at least two-teacher schools, the number of pupils per teacher during the period increased. In some states, the pace of filling posts by the state governments slowed down when OB posts funded by the central government were available. The state

governments also opened new schools without meeting the basic norms, leading to irrational deployment of teachers. Apropos the critical input of teacher training, the DIETs were to restructure and reorganize elementary teacher education to make it more responsive to local needs. But the preliminary results of a study by National Institute of Educational Planning and Administrastion (NIEPA)[77] show that this has not happened. The main reasons are failure to adapt to local conditions and needs; and limited implementation of the underlying idea of the scheme – innovations and experimentation. The DPEP assessmentt[78] also raises the relevant issue of the impact of existing teacher training programs on classroom practice. A large number of teachers have been provided systematic in-service training, and there is some change evident in the use of activities to teach, and in nurturing relationships between teachers and students. But on the whole, training has had only a limited impact on actual classroom experience.

- Discernable connections between performance on project outcomes and unevenness in project implementation: The assessment of DPEP shows that on the count of community involvement, the mobilization of the community and involvement of the Village Education Committees (VECs) in school construction has been successful. But

---

[77] Based on the presentation made by R. Govinda and N. Sood at NIEPA, New Delhi, on May 17, 2000.

[78] World Bank 2003.

this was not true for their participation in, and effect on, improving school quality. Even with the more recent interventions (such as the SSA) that take a decentralized, habitation-based stance, the planning framework is still component and norm-based, making for lack of flexibility. Norms could, in fact, be contextualized, or put into practice flexibly at the ground level, but only if there is capacity building to adapt norms at decentralized levels. Again, with regard to the quality component, textbooks have been revised in several states and the elimination of gender stereotypes have been documented. But this has not yet happened for SC/ST stereotypes; and despite the positive evaluation of textbook content, the evaluation has reportedly been done only in a few states. As far as the planning, conceptualising, and monitoring aspects are concerned, the current focus is on developing state-level institutions to support management and planning of education. Planning has been improved by conceptualizing an annual workplan and budget (AWPB) process. But the role of the AWPB in achieving project outcomes is unclear. Also, the misplaced priority of "enrollment first, quality later" persists, and this has had its effects -the large number of dropouts during Grades 1 and 2. The introduction of Education Monitoring and Information Systems (EMIS) has been an important step to build data systems for planning and monitoring, but these systems need strengthening and incorporation of household data. Research and evaluation, though relatively strong at the national level, is still weak at district and state levels. The literature review reveals that very

---

Primary School Children (6-8 years and 8-11+ years) : Review of Programs

Access: Improved enrollment rates, some reduction in gender disparities but reduction in social disparities not on target, especially in the case of ST children; retention rate target achieved in very few districts. Coverage of AS still less than 5 percent of out-of-school children.

Health/nutrition inputs: MMS proved to be a desirable input; but absence of functional School Health Program in most states a drawback.

Quality: Achievement levels still unsatisfactory, especially for SC children, and even more so for ST children; in-service teacher training and training institutes have not had much impact on classroom practice; textbooks revised, and gender stereotypes reduced, but SC/ST stereotypes continue, and several states have not evaluated textbook content; planning improved by conceptualizing AWPBs, but their role in achieving project outcomes unclear; EMIS introduced to build data systems for planning and monitoring, but needs strengthening and reconciliation with household data; research and evaluation weak at districts and state levels, very little impact evaluation done; financial performance fairly satisfactory, though more detailed analysis required. Poor quality in AS – many of them dysfunctional.

Community involvement: VECs successfully involved in school construction but not in improving school quality.

Priorities for future implementation: Better targeting, improved flexibility, focus on accountability, stronger linkages, and evaluative research and monitoring. Improving access to, quality of, and community participation in alternative schooling and addressing issue of parity with formal schooling.

little impact evaluation has taken place. Finally, financial performance has been fairly satisfactory, though more detailed analysis is required. In sum, the general conclusion of DPEP review is that there are five aspects critical to implementation of future programs: better targeting; improved flexibility; focus on accountability; stronger linkages; and evaluative research and monitoring.

Getting education to the "hard to reach" children- Moving from formal to non-formal education(NFE)/ alternative schooling (AS):

Creating basic learning conditions in alternative schools (AS) is extremely important, as these centers are specially designed to provide the most disadvantaged of children with access to education. AS have helped India take one step ahead in fulfilling her children's fundamental right to education. But these centers continue to experience several problems so that AS are in some danger of being perceived as a poor substitute for formal education. AS centers continue to be plagued by minimal physical facilities, sub-standard and poorly paid instructors, poor conceptual inputs, shorter duration and inconvenient working hours. Their total coverage was, in the late nineties, less than 5 percent of the number of out-of-school children. In fact, evaluation studies carried out by the Operations Research Group (ORG)[79] (in 1994 for Andhra Pradesh and Uttar Pradesh, and 1996 for Lok Jumbish) indicate that a large number of AS centers are dysfunctional. The studies have also identified the factors leading to the

poor performance of AS centers- delays in disbursement of funds and honorarium to instructors; weak training inputs; and lack of interest and commitment of district education officials. Moreover, the overall impact is of poor quality, in terms of both poor infrastructure and less qualified teachers. This is despite the policy intentions of parity with the formal system. The result is that inequities in the system or what are getting to be known as "hierarchies of access", are being exacerbated. The PROBE Survey Report (1999) also added to the list, the absence of community participation and a weak curriculum. In spite of this, says the report, "NFE survives because it is a profitable industry." The AS scheme has, however, now been expanded, with a more flexible design that allows it to be contextualized in the Education Guarantee Scheme and Alternative and Innovative Education. The latter scheme is now a part of the larger *SSA* framework, and is being perceived as a major strategy to bring the "hard to reach" children into the folds of education.

In summary, weighing the pluses and minuses of the situation, and appreciating the commitments and supportive measures of the governments, the inevitable conclusion is that the objective of providing primary level education to all children below the age of 11 has been only partially achieved. The very real achievements are weighed down by several persisting areas of concern — attendance rates, repetition rates, completion rates, quality of schooling and achievement levels, and out-of-school-children, to say nothing of inter and intra-state variations.[80]

---

[79] ORG 1994 and 1996.

[80] School attendance rates are still quite low in states such as MADHYA PRADESH, Rajasthan, Bihar, and Uttar Pradesh.

Not only do many children "attend school" only for a few days in a year, but even when they do attend school, they do not achieve satisfactory learning levels, mainly because of ineffective teaching and failure to cope with the curriculum.[81] The "time on task" provided in the classrooms is often less in a day than that spent doing nothing. The nature of tasks not being stimulating is yet another story.[82] In sum, it is debatable whether children receive an acceptable level of basic education, in terms of basic learning achievements and pedagogical criteria. According to the PROBE survey team, average pupil achievements in Indian schools (especially in government/municipal schools) are extremely low, mainly due to overcrowded classrooms, lack of teaching skills, absence of classroom activity, poor teaching standards and other related deficiencies. Most of all, continued health and nutritional inadequacies hinder the children's use of their chance in school. Thus, it is safe to say that while existing interventions have helped India move closer to the quantitative goal of universal enrollment, the quality issue still remains to be effectively addressed. The quality issue is particularly sharp in the case of disadvantaged communities and deprived regions; their relatively privileged counterparts may be sent to private schools, only to increase the disparity of educational opportunities between the haves and have-nots.

Paving the Way for Change – Analyzing the Poor Impact of Existing Interventions

The thrust of the interventions for the child, as already said, should be on synergy – on the convergence of services and the quality of service delivery – in the context of the development continuum. But the review of programs for the various sub-stages of the child's development – both individually and together – makes it clear that the overall impact has been unsatisfactory. Some concluding remarks in response to these questions are important, particularly in view of India's goal of EFA or SSA targeted for 2010, and MDG (see Chapter 1) by 2015.

In addition to the crucial issue of enough finance and finance management (see Chapter 5), the preceding review of program interventions repeatedly reveals several manifestations of two central aspects of unsatisfactory performance: coverage and quality of service design and delivery.

Coverage:

Poor programmatic impact is directly linked with the context of the beneficiaries. In the case of interventions for the child, we are talking about a context in which the most needy of children, whether poor, rural, female or SC/ST, are not reached; nor are their families and communities; certainly not enough to enable significant participation. The child's needs, and the reciprocal, interactive nature of these needs

---

[81] For instance, a 1999 study of 10 states by the ORG found that among children enrolled in Class 1 in 1992-93, 17 percent were still in Class 1 or 2 six years later. ORG (1999) "Evaluation Study to Assess the Efficiency and Effectiveness of the National Program for Nutritional Support to Primary Education in Ten States of India" Report submitted to UNICEF, New Delhi.

[82] Kaul et al 2003.

as the child grows from one stage of development to the next, demand the holistic view along the age continuum described in this report's conceptual framework. From such a viewpoint, child development cannot separate the analysis and evaluation of educational goals/plans/programs from family welfare in general, and in particular, the health and nutritional needs of children and pregnant/lactating women. In an integrated approach to child development, the continuous process of synergy among the different, yet linked needs of the child's growth, well being, and life choices, must be taken into account. The poverty contexts of target children and their families must be addressed if their gains from school are to be optimized in a convergent mode. It is the absence of this that has resulted in the alienation of potential beneficiaries from existing interventions.

Design and delivery:

From the RCH program to the centrally sponsored education programs such as OB and DPEP, interventions have been centralized and standardized, and almost entirely planned and funded by the central government. Approaches to problems have been compartmentalized. The evaluation of many schemes points to wide gaps between conceptualization and actual implementation, including the lack of holistic planning and convergence between sectors. For example, take the decision to encourage girls' participation in primary education by synchronizing the timings of the ICDS centers and schools. The idea is to provide alternative sibling care facility for the 3-6 year olds, freeing the girls from sibling care. An additional honorarium is paid to the worker for spending longer hours with the children. This decision disregards the fact that the more acute problem for girls is the care of the 0-3 year olds. Also, by involving the worker for longer hours with the children, her other responsibilities — home visits and contact with the lactating mothers — get neglected.

Another example is that of MMS, which operates in several states as a Centrally Sponsored Scheme (CSS), has no coordination with the ICDS operating in the same areas, though both have a nutritional component. This leads to duplication of work and, often, double enrollments. Again, Health Education is a specified curricular area that is expected to be taught in primary schools. Even if MMS is being implemented in the same school, using the meal program as an educational program that will reinforce linked messages of the health education curriculum is not even considered, since the two schemes are viewed as "separate."

The lack of adequate and effective linkages is also a hindrance to an integrated approach. Except for the ICDS, all other programs are stand-alone programs. Evidence shows that there are strong linkages among the components of child development, hence the need for an integrated approach. This is the case with ICDS. But though its design is highly acclaimed, the use of one AWW by ICDS and the expectation that one program will 'do it all' does not appear to be effective, especially when not supported by adequate inputs. Thus, it is clear that the implementation process has to involve greater convergence and rigorous programs for building capacity of implementers at different levels. For these programs to be effective, they have to be held at regular intervals for periodically updating the implementers' skills.

The success of any program depends on the capacity and flexibility of the program and of the implementers to address local demands.[83] The review, however, shows that the quality of delivery has been hampered by weak implementation capacity and an equally weak monitoring system, which are responsible for the tardy functioning of some of the schemes/programs. It is not surprising then to find that large sums allocated to programs have been underutilized. Apart from a thorough review of systems, there should be flexibility in spending, linked to the specific needs of the area and target populations. Various evaluations have shown that most programs tend to be poorly targeted, leading to considerable wastage. Expenditure on children's development, and the areas and ways in which this expenditure takes place, should therefore be a critical part of planning and implementing of programs.

---

[83] Ramachandran et al 2003.

Underwriting the Child's Development

PUBLIC SPENDING ON THE CHILD

▰ Underwriting the Child's Development
Public Spending on the Child

Investing in young children — financially and otherwise — can help "break the vicious intergenerational cycle of poverty in the developing world."

Armeane Choksi 1996.

Trends in Allocations to the Social Sector: The Background of the Nineties[84]

We have seen all along how shortfalls in funds have hindered the achievement of targets in achieving and sustaining the Indian child's development. There is no doubt that the starting point is adequate spending. But increased funding does not necessarily translate into better outcomes for the child; the existing funds, and any future increase in allocations, need to be spent with the maximum efficiency possible.

The public funds allocated to children are classified under four heads: child development, child health, education, and children in difficult circumstances. It should, however, be borne in mind that not only do children have urgent needs for development and education that have to be met with resources; their demands are also a part of an already demanding social sector. Analyzing spending on the overall social sector in the nineties is of particular significance, because this period has been rather unusual in both political and economic terms. Following the acute balance of payment crisis in 1991, the rupee was devalued, and international loans were taken to cope with the immediate problems. A stabilization program was introduced, followed by an adjustment program. "The result has been that the economic development model in 2002 is distinctly different from the development model pursued before 1991. The level of protection is less; the Indian economy has opened up much more to the world market than before."[85]

It is not just the financial climate that has been in the process of transformation. There has also been the shifting nature of definitions, and therefore, of emphases and priorities. Over the years, the perceptions of poverty, poverty alleviation, indices of growth and development have evolved. The conceptualization of poverty became more multidimensional in the 1990s.[86] The central thrust of the concept was now human development, or basic needs interventions; and this thrust was directed at the various aspects that make up the whole person — including health, education, drinking water, housing, roads, food, and empowerment. The concept was also accompanied by an increasing emphasis on participation and new forms of governance.

Social sector allocation as proportion of GDP does not seem to be commensurate with the move towards an emphasis on overall human development.

---

[84] The graphs and tables in this chapter are primarily based on the data provided by government documents, especially the budget documents, and the methodology of compiling the data has drawn profoundly from that of the 2001 HAQ report "India's Children and the Union Budget." The data was analyzed and appropriately updated for this Report by Devendra B. Gupta's 2003 study "Public Spending on Child Development." (See Gupta 2003b.)

[85] Mooij, Jos and S. Mahendra Dev 2002.

[86] Ibid.

This is the conceptual background; the changes in the theoretical background that would drive planning, spending, and project design and implementation. But in practice, the emphasis on human development, and on addressing the many dimensions of poverty, call for sharp increases in allocations to the social sector. The natural question then is, has there been enough spending on the social sector?

An analysis of the Union Government budgets during the nineties shows that throughout the 1990s, social sector expenditure, in terms of percentage of Gross Domestic Product (GDP), was lower than that in the late 1980s.[87] Also, social expenditure in India involves both the center and the states, and the latter were contributing as much as 80 percent to the overall social sector expenditure by 1998-99. Looking at trends within state-level spending, it is apparent that a great deal of expenditure goes to the component of salaries. There are the usual inter-state variations on spending in specific social sectors. For example, Kerala and Punjab spend twice as much on health as Bihar, Madhya Pradesh and Uttar Pradesh do. In fact, these three states show that per capita public spending on health is the lowest in the poorest states.[88] Bringing together these various figures and trends, social sector allocation as proportion of GDP does not seem to be commensurate with the move towards an emphasis on overall human development. This is sharpened by the fact that the social sector has particularly demanding needs from an increasing population – education is just one of the good illustrations of this disparity between available resources and demand. And this inadequacy exists in the picture even before the next logical question is asked: how much of this allocation to the social sector is going to the Indian child?

Recent Patterns of Expenditure on the Child[89]

Again, as in the social sector in general, an analysis of the Union Government budgets during the nineties shows that the increase in spending on children has been marginal.[90] During the nineties, central spending on education and health increased as a percentage of total spending on children as compared to nutrition and early childhood development. A breakdown of the central budget shows that in terms of priority, government spending on children has been highest on education (for instance, in 2001-02, 1.9 percent of the central budget (revised estimates) was allocated for sectoral spending on children; of this more than half (56 percent) was on education alone). The spending on education has almost doubled since the mid-nineties, a period when the government launched many schemes such as DPEP. Within

---

[87] Ibid.

[88] Peters, David et al, World Bank 2002.

[89] The DB Gupta study and the data/graphs by the World Bank team are based on the budget spending calculated on the basis of a methodology adopted from the HAQ Report, 2001. The programs and schemes considered for analysis of the budget for children is based on the HAQ study.

[90] For instance, the actual expenditure increased from Rs 7170 million in 1990-91 to around Rs 30290 million in 2000-01, a four-fold increase in real terms compared to an almost sevenfold increase in nominal terms; and if the increase in population is taken into account, the figure in per capita terms is still lower.

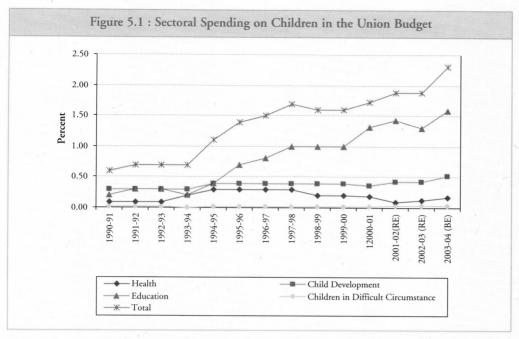

Figure 5.1 : Sectoral Spending on Children in the Union Budget

Source: Demand for Grants, Expenditure Budget Vol. 1 & 2, Union Budget, Government of India, various years.

Note: Covers children from 0-14 age group. The graph shows the expenditure as a percentage of central government (union budget). The last few years are either revised estimates (RE) for 2001-02 & 2002-03 or budget estimates (BE) for 2003-04 of Union budgeting, and the rest are actual estimates (not specified).

education, the share of elementary education is about 50 percent (at the state level, however, there is no such shift towards greater expenditure on elementary education). Meanwhile, external aid for children's programs in the various sectors has increased steeply.[91] On an average, for every 100 rupees spent on children in the 1990s, around 20 rupees came from external aid. Sectorally, external aid on child health is the highest (almost 50 percent).[92] But the share of expenditure on nutrition and early childhood development and on children in difficult circumstances, has remained more or less stationery. It is only for education and health that shares in social sector expenditure have increased (see Figure

5.1). Overall, considering the role that child development plays in the economic and social development of a country, the funds allocated to children appear to be inadequate. And the answer may have to be far more emphatic when we consider the next step in our analysis: how much of the resources allocated to child development actually go the child?

A Closer Look: Spending on Select Child-Related Programs

The funds allocated to children are supposed to reach them through the implementation of programs and schemes planned on their behalf. The ICDS and MMS, as well as primary education programs, are among the most important means designed to benefit the child.

---

[91] From 0.5 percent in 1990-91, to almost 28.7 percent in 1997-98, and 25.9 percent in 1999-2000.

[92] Gupta 2003b.

Trends in ICDS expenditure:

Over the years, absolute spending, as well as the spending per child on various ICDS components, has increased at the national level (see Figure 5.2).[93] Between 1992/93 and 2001/02, both outlays and expenditure on nutrition increased by almost four times. But despite this increase, the actual expenditure on nutrition, as per requirement, for the country as a whole still lags behind. Why? Analyzing trends in ICDS expenditures for the two periods 1992-93 and 2001-02, it is found that operational expenses have increased faster, compared to outlays on SNP, and thus the increase in ICDS allocation has been considerably less in real terms.

Expenditure on SNP is required to be met exclusively by the states. On an average, the state governments spend Rs. 0.51 (year 2001-02) per day per child below the age of six years. Not surprisingly, there are wide inter-state variations: some states spend Rs. 3-5 per day, while many others spend below one rupee. Also, the total ICDS expenditure is almost evenly distributed between operational expenses provided by the center and the supplementary nutrition expenditures incurred by the states. ICDS allocations (central and state governments, 2000-01) as a percentage of their domestic product and revenue expenditure, vary considerably. States such as Andhra Pradesh, Gujarat, Karnataka, Orissa, Punjab, Uttar Pradesh and West Bengal have devoted significant amounts of revenue expenditure to ICDS, but only some of them have performed well, for example in terms of nutrition.

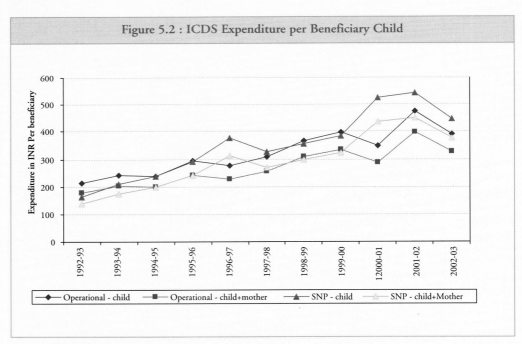

Figure 5.2 : ICDS Expenditure per Beneficiary Child

Source: Demand for Grants, Expenditure Budget , various years

---

[93] The center's increase in contribution rose from Rs 3298 million in 1992-93 to Rs 13112 million in 2001-02. Tamil Nadu, Haryana and Orissa show relatively higher growth rates compared to Bihar and Uttar Pradesh, which show very small or negative growth rates.

Hence, it is difficult to infer that large expenditures on ICDS necessarily contribute to better outcomes; the reasons could be related to program management and larger issues of governance.[94] The actual expenditures exceeded available funds for most states in 1992-93, but the situation changed subsequently, with the states unable to utilize the available funds.[95] The relevant question now is why most states are unable to use, or use in time, the funds available.[96] The possible answers could be delays in the release of funds by the center to the states, and the states' lack of administrative capacity to fully utilize the available funds.

How adequate are the resource allocations vis-a vis, the needs of the state?

Interestingly, a consistent gap is evident between the estimated requirements of funds for a particular state as per population below poverty line and the corresponding departmental estimations and allocations.[97] An analysis of this gap across states categorized on the basis of performance on CDI (refer figure 3.9) shows this gap to be substantially higher in the low CDI states (see Figure 5.3 A). The lower departmental estimations are possibly an artifact of the low absorptive capacity of the states. This phenomenon very likely leads to a vicious cycle of poor endowments and slow development, as indicated in Figure 5.3 B. This suggests a strong case in all projects across sectors for investing concurrently on institutional reforms to ensure both adequacy of financial resources and their efficient use.

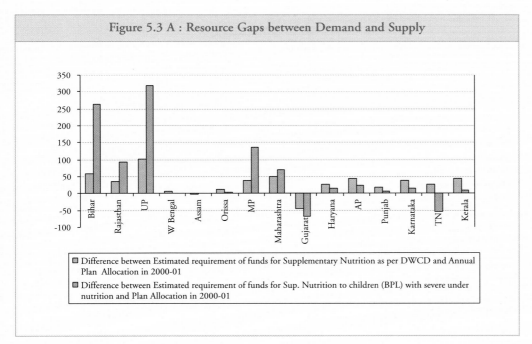

Figure 5.3 A : Resource Gaps between Demand and Supply

■ Difference between Estimated requirement of funds for Supplementary Nutrition as per DWCD and Annual Plan Allocation in 2000-01

■ Difference between Estimated requirement of funds for Sup. Nutrition to children (BPL) with severe under nutrition and Plan Allocation in 2000-01

Source: Annual Report 2001-02, Planning Commission, Government of India

---

[94] ICDS consists of several interventions. To relate outcomes to levels of expenditures, a much more complex analysis will need to be carried out by working out a composite index of outcomes.

[95] In 2001-02, states like Uttar Pradesh, WB, Maharashtra, Gujarat and Karnataka, show low levels of fund utilization.

[96] Southern states have generally performed better in utilization of funds.

[97] Analysis of data from Annual Report of Planning Commission (2001-02)

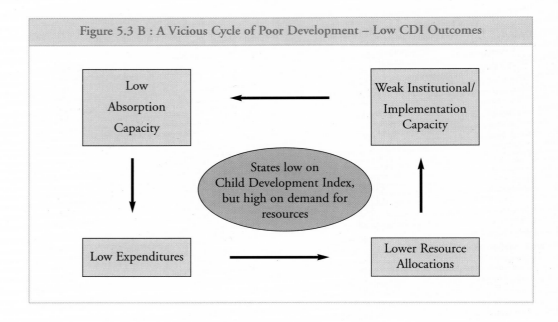

Figure 5.3 B : A Vicious Cycle of Poor Development – Low CDI Outcomes

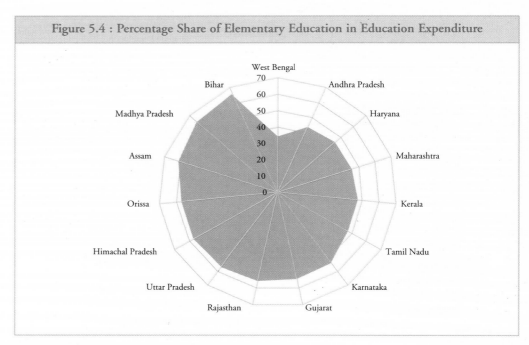

Figure 5.4 : Percentage Share of Elementary Education in Education Expenditure

Source: Analysis of Budget Expenditure on Education, GOI, various years.

Trends in expenditure on elementary education[98] :

It is seen that almost half of government expenditure on education is devoted to elementary education, and that this is especially true of the period from the mid-nineties onwards, with major new initiatives such as DPEP and MMS.

---

98 The data for analysing government expenditure on elementary education is compiled from the Demands for Grants of the Central Ministries and the budget demands of states and Union territories as presented in Parliament/State legislatures. Much of the data analysis in this section is based on Analysis of the Budgetary Expenditure on Education, MHRD, and the Demands for Grants of the same ministry.

Most of the Plan funding comes from the center through CSS (such as DPEP), and state governments continue to do the actual spending, with about 95 percent being spent on salaries. How much does each state actually spend on education per child? The share of elementary education in the total education expenditure varies by state – from a low of 33 percent in West Bengal to a high of 67 percent in Bihar (see Figure 5.4). Though Bihar spends most of its education expenditure on the elementary level, spending per child is not that high. In contrast, Kerala spends less than half of total expenditure on elementary education, but the per student spending is Rs. 500 a year, which is one of the highest figures among the states. So, what matters is not only the proportion of spending, but the actual per-child expenditure.

In sum, the period 1992/93 to 1999/2000 shows an increasing trend in expenditure on elementary education by state, with substantial inter-state variations in growth rates. Overall, there are inter-state differences in the levels and growth of public spending on elementary education. Despite a considerable increase in public spending on elementary education (see Figure 5.5)[99], many states are still far from the universalization goal. Per capita expenditures on elementary education in the low literacy states[100] continue to be lower than those with higher literacy levels, except perhaps Rajasthan. Given the poor financial health of the most educationally backward states, the remedy

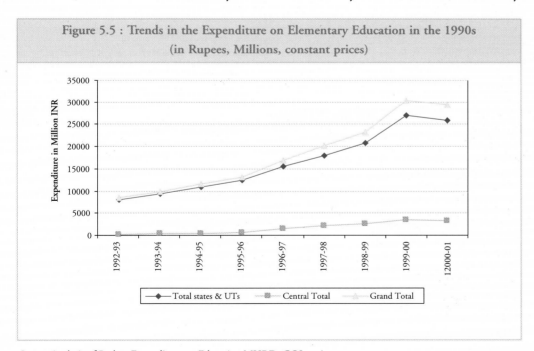

Figure 5.5 : Trends in the Expenditure on Elementary Education in the 1990s (in Rupees, Millions, constant prices)

Source: Analysis of Budget Expenditure on Education,MHRD, GOI, various years

---

[99] The graphs in Figures 5.2 and 5.4 use data adjusted for inflation. The inflation rates used are from the GOI's Economic Survey of India (various years). The Annual Inflation Rates, based on Wholesale Price Index (WPI) taken at a 52 week average for each year, has been used to arrive at inflation-adjusted expenditures.

[100] Bihar, Rajasthan and Uttar Pradesh, for example.

seems to be intervention by the center. By all accounts, the Central Government has stepped up its efforts towards this direction. But an increase in government spending would be fruitless if it is not supported by better management and monitoring.

Trends in expenditure on MMS:

The centrally sponsored National Program for Nutritional Support to Primary Education, also known as MMS, has two principal objectives: boosting universal elementary education (UEE) by improving enrollment and attendance; and enhancing the nutritional status of school children. The number of children covered under the program has increased by almost three times since the launching of the program in 1995-96. About half the expenditure on elementary education is devoted to MMS, whether in current or in constant prices, but despite this earmarked expenditure, the amount of food grains

actually lifted for the meals program lags behind allocation. Also, as usual, there are wide interstate variations, with Rajasthan, West Bengal, Punjab and Gujarat showing poor lifting of food grains.

Taking the Resources to the Child

In all these cases, whether sub-sector and program, it is seen that actual expenditure tends to lag behind the budgetary provision for most years, when comparing what the budget provides for children with what is actually spent on them. For example, over the period for which data is available, the ICDS program, which accounts for almost two-thirds of the allocation for nutrition and early childhood development, shows actual spending on the child falling short of what the budget provides. Another example also has to do with an area where the government allocates relatively substantial funds through its CSSs. The budgeted

> Regardless of program or subsector, actual spending on the child has lagged behind the allocation.

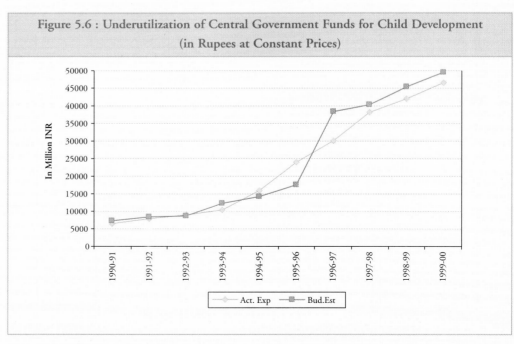

Figure 5.6 : Underutilization of Central Government Funds for Child Development (in Rupees at Constant Prices)

Source: Demand for Grants, Expenditure Budget, various years.

expenditure for elementary education has increased almost 12 times over the decade 1990/91-2000/01, but the actual expenditure has fallen short of the budgetary provision (see Figure 5.6).

What does this pattern of gaps between the budget (such as it is) and the actual spending on the child imply? Considering two of the priority areas: ICDS and elementary education, it has been seen that a substantial component in state-level spending is on salaries, particularly after the Fifth Pay Commission. This is certainly true in the case of ICDS. This is the case again with elementary education, where states are spending on schemes such as DPEP mainly in the form of salaries of all additional teachers and other staff. What happens then to the requirements for educational quality, teacher training and the numerous other components that must be improved to reach the child? The states need to make their contributions to CSSs. In the case of

the SSA, for example, the states are supposed to contribute 25 percent of annual planned expenditure on an incremental basis, but many states may not be in a position to make this contribution. This may be for one or more of the following reasons. It may be because of salary payment, or for the fact that funding the social sector has not been established as a priority. It may be a problem with the release of funds. Sometimes, when funds have been allocated elsewhere, and are unused or have lapsed, these funds are still not diverted to the needy social sector. Or it may simply be the lack of capacity of the agencies implementing the program.

Are resource allocations addressing needs of children holistically?

This research strongly advocates the importance of investing adequately in all sub-stages of childhood, but most particularly in the first 6 years which are the critical formative years for human

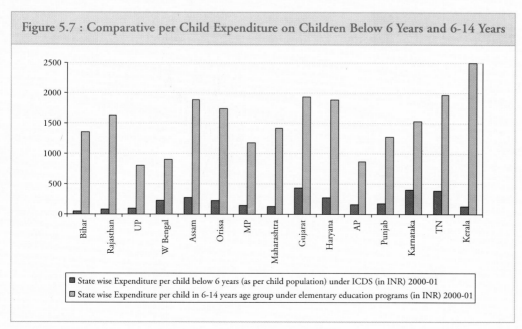

Figure 5.7 : Comparative per Child Expenditure on Children Below 6 Years and 6-14 Years

■ State wise Expenditure per child below 6 years (as per child population) under ICDS (in INR) 2000-01
□ State wise Expenditure per child in 6-14 years age group under elementary education programs (in INR) 2000-01

Source: Calculated from data provided by DWCD and MHRD (2000-01)

development. Investment in these years would also influence the potential of children to benefit from subsequent interventions. The research also makes a case for ensuring that health, nutritional and psycho-social/ educational needs of children are synergistically met.

Are the sub-sectoral allocations for children reflecting this balance? As indicated in Figure 5.7, a comparative analysis of expenditure per child for ICDS and elementary education (which represent the two sub-stages as well as the two sub-sectors of nutrition and education respectively) shows that there is a clear imbalance in favor of the older age group and that too for only education. Per child expenditure on the 6-14 age group is approximately 8 times greater than the per child allocations for below 6 years age group. This imbalance is visible across all states. Its impact can be seen in the fact that improvements recorded over two time periods in CDI in states are

largely contributed to by increase in educational indicators, especially, in enrollments. The lower resources inevitably leads to lower coverage and inadequate targeting, thus reducing the potential for improvement in the status of child development indicators.

Who will speak for the child?

It is this situation – of inadequacy, underutilization and/or inefficient utilization – that leads us to ask the question, who will speak for the child? The other sectors have articulate, sometimes powerful spokespersons, advocating either an increase in fund allocation, or a shift in policy and priority, or an examination of actual spending mechanisms. Children cannot lobby for the resources they need to meet their complex needs. They cannot establish priorities within allocations. In that sense, they have no say in what will be spent on them, when, and how. It is for parents and teachers, for the community, for civil society at large, and for the

decision makers within and outside the government, to turn into spokespersons for children on whom the future of the country rests. It is for them to relate spending on the child to the priority needs of the child at every sub-stage along the development continuum.

Making Changes: The Future of Public Spending on Children

During the nineties, government spending on children increased, and several innovative CSSs were initiated with external assistance, particularly in the areas of child health and primary education.

- But the increase in government spending is only marginal. Despite the increase since the mid-nineties, we still see that less than 2 percent of the Union budget is aimed at children.

- Despite the spending on child health, outcomes have not shown appreciable improvement. Routine immunization, for example, has too often been the poor performer recently.

- Compared to what is needed to achieve universalization, funds have remained scarce. In fact, in real terms, the situation is worse.

- Most of all, there are large inter-state variations. Many of the states where outcome indicators for children are the poorest – Bihar and Uttar Pradesh for instance – also spend less per child on major programs such as ICDS[101] and elementary education. For these

states, the gap between the resources they need and what they get is also much higher. And for most states, operational and administrative costs for programs such as ICDS are higher than what is actually spent on children. Finally, underutilization of allocated funds is an area of serious concern in most states.

What next?

There can be no two opinions that we have to give voice to the child's needs by pushing for more spending and better spending on children. It goes without saying that any budget is only as good as the way it is actually spent; on the people it reaches and the needs it actually meets. So how to increase the budget, and make spending on children more efficient? First, there is the inevitable need to increase the resources available for the priority needs of Indian children, particularly in the below 6 years age group. The Working Group Report of the Tenth Five Year Plan (2002-07) expresses concern that the actual provision for ICDS was less than the approved outlay during the Ninth Five Year Plan. This meant not only delays in operationalizing the projects, but also, in some cases, inadequate release of funds to state governments. In terms of priorities, the Plan acknowledges that one of the lessons learnt from the Ninth Five Year Plan experience is that addressing "the whole child" is more cost-effective than individual services delivered separately, thus making a case for child-budgeting.[102]

---

[101] Low per capita expenditure on ICDS is shown by Bihar, Chattisgarh, Madhya Pradesh, Andhra Pradesh, Rajasthan and Uttar Pradesh – states plagued by low birth weight babies, high MMRs, and high malnutrition levels.

[102] Working Group Report on Child Development, Tenth Five Year Plan, GOI 2001h.

Also, on the subject of priorities, the emphasis should be on playing the role of developer of human resources, not the provider of hardware or infrastructure. The focus needs to be widened to include the urban marginalized. For example, as many as 40 percent of the deprived children ICDS should be reaching reside in urban slums and other poor urban areas. One of the most crucial aspects of prioritizing spending on child development is, necessarily, establishing who needs more spending as soon as possible, and on which basic needs. In other words, resources have to be earmarked for the benefit of the most needy – the disadvantaged children (girls, SC/ST children, rural children, out-of-school or working children, and children with disabilities) Given the link between child and mother, these priorities have to include, in as seamless a package as possible, the health, nutrition, and awareness needs of the pregnant, lactating, and child-rearing mother. The other guiding principle to be kept in mind when it comes to spending on the child is that the platitude "a stitch in time saves nine" is valuable in the context of child development. Spending on the early years of the child's life means addressing in good time the possible accumulation of deficits as the child grows. Instead, such spending promotes an accumulation of gains that support further development rather than hindering it. Thus, the investment yields the best sort of returns – cumulative, sustained returns.

In the ultimate analysis, increased allocations and financial reform, however desirable, will not make for real, beneficial spending on the child. It is simply a matter of increasing the efficiency of spending. This is where better targeting comes in, given the fact that it is the most needy and marginalized and out-of-reach children who need to benefit if the overall situation is to improve. Again, this is where administrative reform and good governance also come in. Take education for instance. Good governance is crucial in various inputs required for improved quality, from teacher recruitment to accountability. What are the factors that inhibit good governance? Lack of transparency, personnel problems and performance incentives all come to mind. IEC are indispensable means to change behavior, and they need to be built into projects to deliver messages, conduct research and monitor impact.[103] IEC needs more resources allocated for the purpose, and the implementation of these IEC programs also needs to be improved. If the management of resources for children is to be made more effective, complementary changes in management practices, work routines, and career development policies – including incentives for staff to get more training – will help to permanently modify the behavior of field workers. Performance-based budgeting, which links disbursements to performance, would engage implementing agencies in designing and managing programs and increasing accountability in terms of outcomes.[104]

---

[103]Healthcare in India: Learning from Experience, OED, Number 187, World Bank 1999c.
[104]Ibid.

The Way Ahead
MAJOR CONCERNS
AND RECOMMENDATIONS

The Way Ahead
Major Concerns and Recommendations

Getting Ready for Action: The Background of Priorities

Throughout the review, this research has addressed some critical questions about the present situation. Are our children ready for school? And are our schools ready for our children? Are the family and community fully supportive of children's needs and rights? The answers to all these questions have been "Not yet" or "Not enough." In which case, what is the way ahead?

The review of the current situation has identified certain priorities for action for every sub-stage along the development continuum. These include antenatal care; complete immunization; nutritional security of children as well as of expectant and lactating mothers; pre-schooling; and retention in and completion of primary school with satisfactory learning levels. Side by side, the review of existing interventions indicates that the priority areas for program improvement are: targeting of the most needy states, communities and children; changes in design and priorities; quality of service delivery; efficiency in the use of human and financial resources; effective health and nutrition education; and greater community involvement. Overall, the issue that has to be addressed is helping children enter and regularly attend school, successfully negotiate the lower primary grades and, having completed the cycle, emerge as well educated and healthy children. The Tenth Five-Year Plan has set targets for child development and education that are even more ambitious

"Because human capital is an investment good, it is important to account for the life cycle dynamics of learning and skill acquisition in devising effective policies. Schooling is only one phase of a lifetime skill accumulation process. Families, firms and schools all create human capital. Any comprehensive analysis of human capital policy must account for the full range of institutions that produce it."

Carnerio and Heckman 2003

than the MDG. These targets, in fact, reflect the government's sense of urgency in pushing the indicators in the right direction. There are also the recent demonstrations of political will to change this situation – with, for example, the recent constitutional amendment that makes elementary education a fundamental right, or with the setting up of the National Mission for Nutrition. In this context, it is both timely and essential to determine the way ahead: whether there is a need to do "more of the same thing" for the Indian child, or whether there is a need to change track. This chapter provides some ideas and recommendations in this context.

Moving Ahead: Changing the Policy Paradigm

The analysis shows that there has to be a change in the policy paradigm informing the planning of interventions for the Indian child. In which case, what should the direction be?

Broadly, the research recommends a move towards:

- An outcome-focused and child-centered approach to planning for children

- A multi-sectoral approach

- A demand-driven, community based,business plan approach
- Contextualized, decentralized planning
- Improved targeting and monitoring
- Improved service delivery
- Making the private sector more accountable and forging new partnerships
- Better use of information, education and communication to mobilize the community and raise awareness
- Greater investment in the very young child
- Targeting public financing for poor children

From an input focus towards an outcome-focused and child-centered approach to planning for children:

Based on a review of international and Indian research, and vetted through a process of active dialogue with Indian professionals across sectors, this research has contributed an Indian conceptual framework for integrated child development that adopts a child-centered approach. The framework's perspective of child development outcomes and determinants is integrated and holistic and reinforces the message that child development outcomes are essentially inter-dependent. This perspective applies both laterally – across health, nutrition, and education/psychosocial development – and vertically, through the different sub-stages of development from the prenatal stage to the end of the childhood period at 11+ years. Guided by such a perspective, the framework argues for the extension of child development concerns beyond the conventional periods of prenatal to six

years to prenatal to 11+ years to cover the entire childhood period. And given the synergistic relationship among health, nutrition and psychosocial development, the framework presents the successful completion of primary education as an appropriate marker for integrated child development. The framework's holistic approach makes it imperative for interventions to reach the child at the critical early stage of life, and then ensure that the child crosses each sub-stage of development continuum successfully, in terms of the identified outcomes, to reach the major milestone of successful completion of primary education.

Thus, the integrated conceptual framework calls for planning that

- Addresses the continuous and cumulative nature of child development, and recognizes the need to intervene in every stage of child development – since what precedes influences the quality of what follows;
- Recognizes the priority needs of each sub-stage of child development; and
- Emphasizes the synergistic, interdependent and complementary nature of health, nutrition, education and psychosocial development that operates within the dynamics of the child's proximal and distal environment.

It is clear that the child, and child-related outcomes, must at all times remain the central focus of planning. *To ensure the achievement of child-related outcomes, the research strongly recommends locating the planning and monitoring of programs for young children within a comprehensive and holistic child development framework such as the one developed.* The review of policies and programs has revealed that over the last few Plan periods, there has been considerable talk of "child-centered approaches" in child development and education, and of the Lifecycle Approach in programs for children. These views have been further articulated and endorsed by the Tenth Five Year Plan.

But in practice, the different sub-stages of childhood and their priorities continue to be addressed in a fragmented, discrete way. Not surprisingly, the status of Indian children vis-à-vis development indicators remains unsatisfactory. For example take an integrated program such as the ICDS, which caters to children below the age of six, covering two sub-stages – prenatal-3 and 3-6 years. The ICDS experience has been that the pendulum of priority often swings from one sub-stage to another or from one aspect of development to another, to the ultimate detriment of both. The result is that the priorities in each sub-stage do not get addressed comprehensively; nor do all the aspects of development, from nutrition and health or to ECCE. Again, child mortality is a health issue, but the implications of reduction in child mortality for future enrollments are rarely discussed. Similarly, though there is empirical evidence that ECCE makes a difference of almost 15-20 percent to the continuation of children in primary school, elementary education planning does not take this finding into account. Though child labor is perceived as a significant deterrent to the probability of children completing their schooling, it is not necessarily included in planning for bringing children into school, since child labor is so often seen as the responsibility of another department.

In its study of a child-centered approach, the research brings out the message: child development outcomes are clearly inter-dependent and the factors that determine child development, are clearly not just in the classroom, or only in the primary school. The research review also reveals the complex system of relationships that act on the child (see Figure 2.9 ,Chapter 2). In the innermost circle is the child with her mother or caregiver. This makes responding to the intersecting needs of children and women critical. Programs for women's empowerment and girls' education need to take into account the conditions necessary for their participation, including alternative childcare facilities that will free them for active participation. Recent evidence of the positive effects of relocating ECE centers in primary schools and synchronizing their timings in DPEP program were seen in terms of enhancing the participation of girls in primary education. But unfortunately, such initiatives are not easily sustained beyond the project stage because of the "compartmentalized thinking" of the nodal departments involved. With ample evidence from around the globe of the significant relationship between mothers' education and child development indicators, a focus on women's literacy, linked with economic independence, is likely to have multiple benefits for the family, and in turn for the child. This makes a case for the convergence of child development programs with programs for women's literacy and empowerment.

Beyond the mother, caregiver and family, there is the neighborhood; the larger system of health services; and finally, in the outermost circle, the general cultural environment, which either reinforces or erodes values, customs and practices. All these elements are significant. Within and between each circle, there is dynamic movement, and as a result, development is not static. Which is why, child development concerns need to go beyond "the individual child" to the total context of the child within and outside the family. All the significant factors in the child's proximal and distal environments are potent influences on the child's development. As a result, a few hours in the anganwadi or school cannot ensure optimal development unless the total context of the child is also conducive and congenial. The child's physical environment, including the availability of clean water and sanitation, must also be catered to if the child's health and physical well-being are to be part of her "whole" development.

From a sectoral approach to a multi-sectoral approach:

The overall message of the research is clear: *child development and early education have to be approached in a comprehensive, multi-sectoral and integrated way.* But this certainly does not mean that any single model or any single integrated program can meet all the comprehensive needs of children. Such a strategy, besides being unfeasible, would also be highly counter-productive. A clear example is the ICDS program that caters to several developmental needs of children across the prenatal-6 age group. It is seen from the review of programs that although the ICDS is now in its 30th year of implementation, it has not been able to demonstrate significant impact due to several problems. There is the major

problem of overloading the *AWW* with an unrealistic number of responsibilities (see Box 4.3). There are also the problems of inadequate personnel preparation to handle cross-sectoral information and challenges; inadequate convergence with other sectors; inadequate infrastructure; over-standardization of design; and shifting priorities. Learning from these experiences, how else is the desired multi-sectoral approach to be operationalized?

First and foremost, *by mapping priorities across current schemes/ sectors.* This research has clearly established the significance of identifying priorities for each sub-stage along the child development continuum. Once the priorities are identified, they require comprehensive and strategic planning to be met. Such planning would have to begin with analyzing and answering four significant questions at all levels of planning:

- What are the development and educational outcomes the community desires for children at every sub-stage – outcomes that will enhance the probability of children successfully completing their basic schooling and improving their life chances?

- What are the necessary conditions and interventions for the realization of the expected outcomes?

- Which scheme or sector has the comparative advantage of delivering these conditions?

- How can the status of these outcomes be assessed/monitored regularly?

These questions require serious examination if we are to avoid doing "more of the same thing." A specific example:

providing ECCE is a priority for children between the ages of three and six, both as a foundation for life-long development and as a preparation for schooling. The relevant question is, should the responsibility for providing ECCE be located in DWCD or does Department of Education (DOE) have the comparative advantage of providing this service more efficiently?

On the basis of lessons learnt, this review recommends that DWCD should take responsibility for crèches and play centers for prenatal-3 year olds, and DOE greater responsibility for ECCE programs for the 3-6 year olds. At present, ECCE is the mandate of DWCD, which routes delivery largely through the ICDS program, which it administers. The current situation, we have seen, is that only 15-20 percent of children in this age group avail themselves of any kind of ECE, although the ICDS program is being universalized. The probable reason for this underutilization is that the pre-school component of ICDS centers is very weak, particularly in the northern states, and they tend, as a consequence, to be perceived as nutrition centers. But evaluation studies of experiments carried out in DPEP have consistently indicated that compared to the habitation-based ICDS model, DPEP's school-based ECCE model is more suited to the delivery of school readiness to 3-6 year olds. The DPEP model promotes early bonding with school – most children are enthusiastic about accompanying their older siblings to school. The model also ensures greater continuity in terms of the curriculum. A school-based ECCE center also enables older girls to participate in schooling because it frees them from sibling care responsibility. But the habitation based ICDS model is less

able to deliver ECE to this age group because of limited space and an overload of cross-sectoral demands on the *Anganwadi Worker (AWW)*, to say nothing of the lower priority given to this component and its monitoring. In fact, the ICDS model is better suited to children below the age of three because the needs of children at this stage are relatively less structured, which an *AWW* can easily handle in addition to her other responsibilities. Also, the proximity of the center to the family and easier access for younger children is an advantage. This differential perspective becomes even more relevant considering the current emphasis on shifting the ICDS priority to nutrition for children under the age of 3 years. It is noted that despite thirty years of intervention, the issue of malnutrition remains very much in the picture, and continues to have an adverse impact on optimal child development. There is also a high level of vulnerability to malnutrition among the under-threes, since this age is the "growth faltering" sub-stage. In other words, while the nutrition input is a priority during the growth-faltering sub-stage of prenatal-3 years, ECE is the priority input for 3-6 year olds. Of course, both nutrition and ECE need to be mapped as important in any planning for children.

There is a shift of emphasis in ICDS towards nutrition, particularly among the under-threes. The Tenth Five Year Plan also indicates nutrition to be the priority for the under-threes but it does not indicate how the ICDS will handle this priority while continuing with its responsibility to different stakeholders, including the 3-6 year olds. This need for balancing existing responsibilities with the new ones becomes particularly sharp if no additional features – extra staffing and resources for example – are addressed. The program can hardly place all its hopes in community participation. Thus, while the intention is well articulated, the operational aspects remain weak.[105] If existing schemes do not have the required conditions for success, alternative interventions must be planned. Finally, planning must be realistic if it is to make a difference to the lives of Indian children.

From a supply-driven to a demand-driven, community based business plan approach:

The traditional schematic supply-driven approach typically adopts a standardized model across the country, a model comprising discrete components, and stringent norms that disregard contextual and cultural diversities. The current ICDS and the educational programs prior to DPEP are specific examples. Reaching the desired outcome demands a move from such an approach to a more demand-based, bottom-up approach that reflects community needs and priorities. *This shift in terms of planning and implementation of programs may be seen as a shift from the traditional approach in developing a process for action to a business plan approach.* The traditional approach is based on:

- Needs assessment (describing the nature and depth of the problem);

- Goals and objectives (vision and values, proposed outcomes);

- Program description (description of activities and service delivery mechanisms);

- Work plan (steps to implement, budget); and

- Evaluation at the conclusion of the project.

The business plan approach, on the contrary would entail:

- Market description (definition of geographic and needs based description of the market at whom the product/service is directed);

- The numbers in the market the products are designed to reach;

- The characteristics of the program or service;

- Performance targets and consequences (tangible results which the program or service will achieve);

- Product and advantages (services, evidence that the product/service will achieve intended results, comparative advantage over other product/services);

- Milestones (process and content outcomes, strategic plan for resource generation);

- Project management (governance, management, and administrative systems critical to success); and

- Learning and development (methods to make course corrections and continuously improve performance).

From centralized, standardized planning to contextualized, decentralized and convergent planning – Preparing Village Plans for Children:

The key to contextualized planning is decentralizing the planning process, while

---

[105]Heywood 2003.

allowing for a transition period of training and support. Such a period will enable adequate capacity building for identifying issues and formulating area-specific plans at the sub-state level. In the education sector, DPEP was the first program to focus on district-based planning, and to bring in some degree of contextualized planning. But, over the project period, there was clear evidence of the need for capacity enhancement. At the same time, given the reality of wide diversities, DPEP experience highlighted the need to move further down to the level of the habitation, making it the unit of planning. This lesson has been incorporated in the *SSA* program, the DPEP's successor. Taking the move in this direction still further, this report recommends moving away from the traditional sectoral plans for education, health and nutrition separately to *preparing multi-sectoral and convergent Village Plans for Children, within the framework of the existing schemes.*

Experience shows that convergence is more possible and sustainable when combined with an area-intensive approach at decentralized levels. The current shift in many states towards the *Panchayat Raj* system especially in the social sector is likely to allow greater space for this convergence and for decentralized planning. Thus, a village plan for children will enable comprehensive outcome-based planning, focused on a specific geographical area and an identifiable target group. In such a situation, all provisions will converge in a consistent and complementary way to promote the development of children in the prenatal-11 age group in that area. This will allow for more systematic monitoring of outcomes, greater responsiveness to contextual diversities, more community participation, and greater efficiency in the use of resources. Such a Plan would draw on existing schemes across sectors to focus on the specific and contextual needs of children across the health, nutrition and education sectors, and along the entire childhood development continuum. This would, to some extent, extend the model of the District Elementary Education

Plans envisaged by the *SSA* program from a unisectoral to a multi sectoral one. The Village Plan for Children would involve a move from a norm-based approach to a more flexible one, which allows for greater community involvement and ownership. Thus, the community will receive sufficient incentive – the welfare of its children – to ensure that service provision is implemented, and implemented well.

However, for such a decentralized approach to be put into operation, schemes for children will have to move away from a norm-based, inflexible design to a more flexible model that allows for greater autonomy at decentralized levels. More autonomy must be backed up by provision for open-ended block grants and performance-based incentives, as well as increased accountability, focused on outcomes. Locating an experienced nodal person (from among existing community based functionaries or an existing NGO) who could be trained as a Child Facilitator to work closely with *panchayat* members and other representatives of the community to enable the process of preparing village plans in a participatory mode would be useful. This Child Facilitator could be a woman at the *panchayat* level – a community coordinator, a member of an established NGO, or a member of a local body like the mothers' committees formed by the ICDS in Andhra Pradesh.

The possibilities of recasting existing programs using the experience of recent elementary education programs (such as DPEP and *SSA*) could also be considered, so as to incorporate a decentralized and flexible approach. This applies, for instance, to the RCH program and the ICDS, both of which continue to be centralized in terms of planning. This is also particularly relevant given the possibility of having to operationalize the recommendations of this report without any imminent financial enhancement.

Keeping this in mind, Figure 6.1 suggests a possible structure within the existing administrative arrangements, to prepare and operationalize these decentralized, child-centered village plans.[106] There is a two-way, dynamic process visualized in operation here. First, from the bottom-up perspective, there is the local level, at which the VEC, the *panchayat* and the mothers' group or Parent Teachers' Association could be coordinated by a Child Facilitator or an NGO to design the basic plans in accordance with the local children's contextualized needs and targets. These would address needs of children along the continuum i.e. from Pre natal to 11+ years. This planning needs to be done in consultation with the larger community, through, for example, a device such as the *Lok Sampark Abhiyan* (People's Contact Program). These plans could be put together at the *panchayat* level first, then vetted and aggregated at the cluster level. The plans are further aggregated, and prioritized for convergence, at the block level. Next, at the district level, the block plans are in turn aggregated, prioritized and also categorized according to

---

[106]This is an extended version of a model already under elementary education in Madhya Pradesh, and, to some extent, in many states under *SSA*.

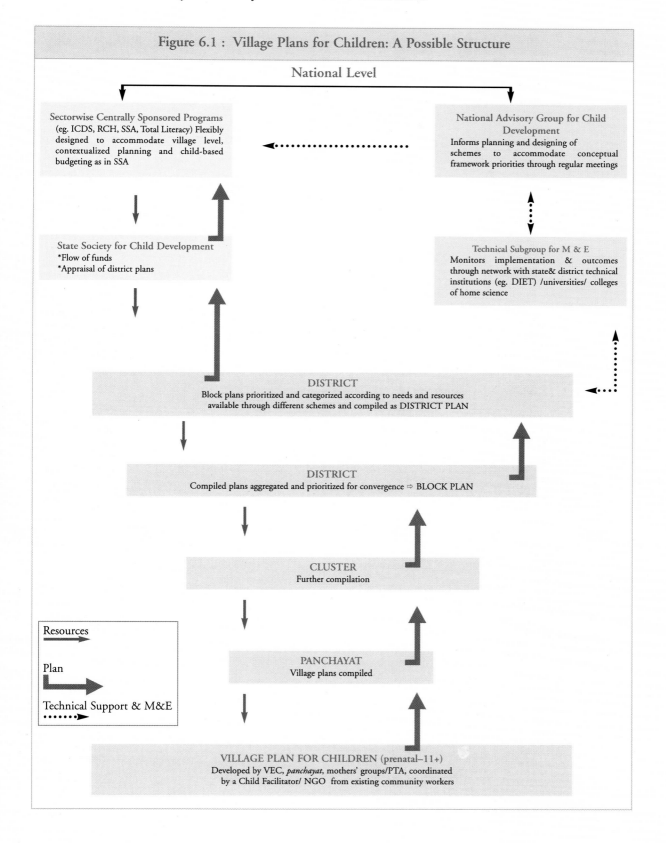

Figure 6.1 : Village Plans for Children: A Possible Structure

National Level

Sectorwise Centrally Sponsored Programs (eg. ICDS, RCH, SSA, Total Literacy) Flexibly designed to accommodate village level, contextualized planning and child-based budgeting as in SSA

National Advisory Group for Child Development
Informs planning and designing of schemes to accommodate conceptual framework priorities through regular meetings

State Society for Child Development
*Flow of funds
*Appraisal of district plans

Technical Subgroup for M & E
Monitors implementation & outcomes through network with state& district technical institutions (eg. DIET) /universities/ colleges of home science

DISTRICT
Block plans prioritized and categorized according to needs and resources available through different schemes and compiled as DISTRICT PLAN

DISTRICT
Compiled plans aggregated and prioritized for convergence ⇨ BLOCK PLAN

CLUSTER
Further compilation

PANCHAYAT
Village plans compiled

Resources

Plan

Technical Support & M&E

VILLAGE PLAN FOR CHILDREN (prenatal–11+)
Developed by VEC, *panchayat*, mothers' groups/PTA, coordinated by a Child Facilitator/ NGO from existing community workers

the needs and resources available through different central and state schemes. *Thus, the district level becomes the meeting point between the bottom-up and top-down movement of the planning and implementation process.*

As far as the top-down perspective is concerned, there are sector-wise centrally sponsored scheme such as the RCH, ICDS and *SSA*, of which the latter, for the most part, is envisaged as flexible enough to accommodate decentralized planning. In addition, there are also several state schemes promoting children's development. These flexibly designed schemes to accommodate village-level contextualized planning and child-based budgeting would be routed through a multi-sectoral and autonomous State Society for Child Development set up under the direct administrative control of the Chief Minister, so as to avoid conflict among line departments. Figure 6.1 visualizes the percolation of funds from the national level through the Society to the sub district levels, in response to district plans for children that emanate from the district and sub district levels. The proposed structure also visualizes the setting up of a National Advisory Group for Child Development, which would be responsible for informing policy planning and the design of schemes to accommodate the priorities of the conceptual framework. This Group would be similar to the Working Groups for the five-year plans, but unlike those groups, which are short-termed, it will be an ongoing one. The Group will be supported by a separate unit for monitoring and evaluation – a technical committee such as the erstwhile Central Technical Committee of the ICDS, which can take the lead in monitoring and evaluation by, for instance, conducting sample-based evaluation studies through a network of state-and district-level technical institutions. The results of the monitoring exercises would feed into the National Advisory Group, and with feedback from each level in the structure, the National Advisory Group would be able to fulfill its responsibility of evidence-based planning and designing of schemes. Experimenting with the Village Plans for Children through district pilots in one state would be the best possible start. Such pilots would need to include a rigorous evaluation component to gauge feasibility and impact, before the plans are scaled up.

For this decentralized approach to be effective, an essential condition would be the devolution of much greater autonomy and freedom of choice at the existing decentralized, community levels. The ultimate vision guiding this concept of community ownership is to have block funds made available to local communities which would enable them to choose and 'buy' services from the line bureaucracies, or NGOs or the private sector locally to address their plans for their children. The accountability would be in terms of their responsibility for the identified and agreed outcomes. However, this change over to total autonomy will have to be gradual, given the current centralized arrangements and schemes with the line ministries and the resistance to change.

For effecting this transition, some measures could be considered. One possibility for bringing in a natural convergence and accountability in the current system could be to issue 'child development progress cards' for every child from 0-11+ years, by the local *Panchayat* or School Management Committee. This card could track children's progress across some prioritised cross-sectoral indicators agreed with the community, such as birth weight, immunization, nutritional level, pre-school participation etc. leading upto school completion. These cards could then be collated to report on the Village / Ward child development status and publicized and/or further aggregated into the CDI.

Thus, if Plan targets are to be achieved, greater decentralization and horizontal linkages across various programs will make for more effective outreach. Operationalizing a convergent approach thus requires:

- The mapping of priorities;

- The identification of comparative strengths and joint planning across programs and sectors;

- Increasing the flexibility of existing institutional arrangements so that they adapt to the partnership, coordination and convergence mode from sub-district and district levels to state and national levels;

- Initiatives for institutional and policy reform, particularly in the area of decentralization and devolution of autonomy and funding to local governments;

- Better, more field based training from a multi-sectoral perspective; and

- Inter-sectoral convergence mechanisms, such as joint planning and monitoring committees at all levels of administration, which assume a more proactive role in overseeing programs.

Improving targeting and Monitoring:

Throughout this report, we have seen that programs in the social sector have not been able to reach the "hardest to reach" states and groups to the extent required by the current situation. For instance, recent studies on the major programs for children (ICDS and DPEP) have indicated the need for better targeting of the "difficult to reach" groups who should be the main beneficiaries of these schemes (see Figures 6.2 and 6.3).[107] Thus, resources and interventions have to be focused on the most nutritionally and educationally vulnerable groups, as well as the geographical pockets in the country that are the most insecure, as far as the needs of children and women are concerned. Figure 6.2 shows, that SC children are relatively more vulnerable for age-appropriate weight in states such as Haryana and Orissa, and ST children in states such as Andhra Pradesh, Rajasthan and West Bengal. This calls for interventions that focus on health, nutrition and hygiene education and practices, a robust school health program, a hot midday meal, and access to safe water and sanitation. Similarly, Figure 6.3 shows pockets of disadvantages in various states for age-specific enrollment in primary schools for 6-11 year-old children (also see Fig 3.9 depicting the comparative status of states on the CDI). Again, the importance of a contextualized

---

[107] Heywood 2003, Ramachandran et al 2003, Gupta 2003b.

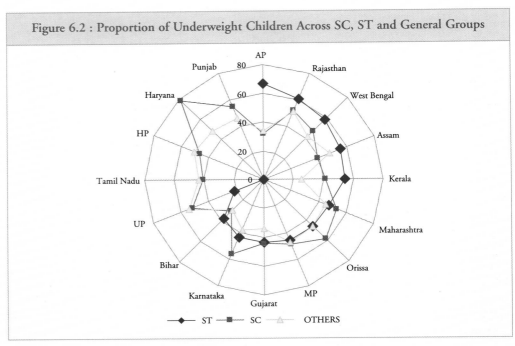

Figure 6.2 : Proportion of Underweight Children Across SC, ST and General Groups

Source: Indicus Analytics 2003 – Analysis of NFHS II (1998-99)

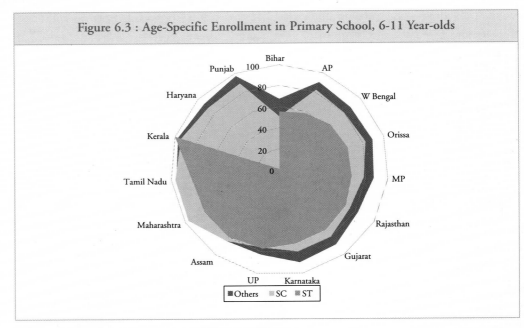

Figure 6.3 : Age-Specific Enrollment in Primary School, 6-11 Year-olds

Source: Indicus Analytics 2003 – Analysis of NFHS II (1998-99)

approach to the needs of these groups cannot be overestimated. On the basis of these findings, this report concludes that *interventions need to be scaled up state-wise and targeted to reach the most needy, in* *consistence with the situation in that state — "pockets of disadvantage," whether these consist of ST children, SC children, girls, and children from urban slums.*

For better targeting of services and provisions to the states and groups that need it most, systems of monitoring and evaluation also need to be improved. This is especially applicable to the availability and reliability of data, and the capacity at all levels to use this data meaningfully. Many sources of household data are available at present, including the 2001 Census data. Many states have also computerized household census data covering every child, and it is expected that this will be documented in a Village Education Register. Where available, the census and household data would facilitate the identification of vulnerable groups – child labor, girls, tribals, poor children – and their needs. If reliable, these data sets will also enable a system of child tracking and child specific interventions as a part of the proposed Village Plan for children. In keeping with this, the Report recommends close attention to promotion of data use and data quality; and suggests sensitization to the relevant issues so as to change attitudes, and enhance capacity at the community level.

Improving service delivery:

We have identified the key areas for service delivery for children as the availability and quality of prenatal and antenatal care, immunization, responsive feeding and care, pre-school education and primary education – the last particularly in terms of completion rates and satisfactory levels of learning. The poor impact of provisions for antenatal care, for example, could be due to low availability or utilization, particularly in remote areas; and this could be linked to the poor quality of care provided. Another example of the impact

of poor quality of services is pre-school education; the demand for the kind of pre-school education currently provided seems low. The qualitative case studies found that the pre-school component of ICDS, for example, is particularly poor[108] and it is seen from the analysis of data[109] that levels of pre-school enrollment are very low (see Figure 3.5). Both the availability and quality of pre-school education need to improve dramatically, given the importance of cognitive stimulation among the 3-5 year-old age group. There has been more success in providing preventive health services such as immunization, IFA tablets, and Vitamin-A supplementation. There has been a considerable increase in their outreach, though more needs to be done to reach the entire targeted population.

The research review shows that weak implementation capacity and an equally weak monitoring system, coupled with over centralization, are responsible for the tardy functioning of some of the schemes/programs. It is not surprising then to find that large sums allocated to programs have been underutilized. *Roles, especially at the grassroots level, need to be clarified and rationalized, particularly in the case of ICDS.* One consequence will also be greater ease in dealing with the complementarity of specified roles so as to avoid duplication and facilitate more outcome-focused interventions. This applies both to the complementarity of the roles specified for *AWWs* and ANMs, and to the complementarity of their roles and those of school teachers. Apart from a thorough

---

[108]Ramachandran et al 2003.

[109]Indicus Analytics 2003.

review of systems, spending has to be made more flexible and linked to the specific needs of the area and target populations. Various evaluations have shown that most programs tend to be poorly targeted, leading to considerable wastage.

The issue of quality of service delivery invariably leads to certain issues of governance. *Evid*ence of these factors in operation is apparent in the case studies in Uttar Pradesh, Karnataka and Andhra Pradesh – in the differential quality of the same programs implemented in different states Experience shows that services for children, whether through the *Anganwadi* or the primary school, get utilized and owned by the community only to the extent that the service delivered is perceived to be of value by the community. On the other hand, quality on such a large scale can only be assured through greater community *involvement, oversight and ownership. This vicious cycle of poor quality leading to less community involvement, needs to be broken through by addressing quality of service delivery in terms of (a)* understanding and influencing the nature of community demand and identifying and ensuring basic conditions for quality – be it in a school, or *anganwadi* including physical facilities, effective local leadership, rationalization of roles and responsibilities for example of an *anganwadi* worker, the ANM and school teachers; (b) setting conditions for meeting the community's right to information and transparency through social audit; for example putting up information regarding the devolved funds to school committees on the school notice board, as in DPEP or publishing education grants to school

districts in Ugandan newspapers and developing community ownership of the service offered; (c) educating the community, particularly the poor, to empower them as citizens to bring pressure on the administrators and politicians to improve services for children; for example, the Bangalore Citizen report cards or the use of media to regularly publish stories of success and failures in service delivery in Andhra Pradesh; (d) by bringing in greater focus on outcomes through, for instance, maintaining and publicizing aggregated information from the child development report cards- for *panchayat*s to make them more accountable; and (e) introducing some incentive mechanisms, monitory or related to the career ladder, to reward performance and motivate the frontline workers.

In this context it is also important to put the child development interventions into the agenda of local politicians to bring in collective accountability. In a recent initiative,[110] Madhya Pradesh Government has done this for accountability in terms of education-related outcomes. Such an initiative has a lot of potential, and other states could explore the possibility of initiating similar interventions for education, as well as all the child development indicators.

Making the private sector more accountable and forging new partnerships:

The case studies indicate that medicines for children are bought off the shelf in an environment devoid of regulation. In fact, one particular child interviewed reports

---

[110]The Jan Shiksha Adhiniyam, or People's Education Act.

that when he is sick, he buys a "fever pill" in the village shop and treats himself![111] The same absence of regulation is evident in the case of pre-primary as well as primary schools that have proliferated in recent years to provide "miseducation" for a fee. This is particularly true of ECE, and the implications – of what an early "education" that is not child-sensitive and developmentally appropriate does to the child's development – hardly needs to be described. Thus, whether it is the reality of "health" being bought across the counter, or private schools being sought after because of a perception of better quality, the reality of the private sector presence needs to be officially acknowledged. *This is necessary in order that there can be adequate and appropriate regulation, whether through direct government intervention (which has its attendant problems) or more effectively through making the community more vigilant and informed as consumers, through an effective IEC initiative.*

The quality of service delivery also requires taking on the issue of *forging new institutional arrangements and partnerships.* Next, though it obviously bears the central responsibility of catering to the Indian child's needs, the public sector needs additional partners – from the business community and the IT sector, to NGOs, NRIs, institutions and professional bodies. There are numerous examples today of partnerships between the corporate sector and the government in improving quality of public services. The Learning Guarantee Scheme in Karnataka, the support program to

municipal schools provided by some NGOs across the country, and the involvement of the Rotary Club and other social organizations in promoting the immunization of children are a few examples. Needless to say, partnerships such as these must be backed by sound professional advice and support to ensure quality.

Community participation will, in all likelihood, invest programs with the kind of enthusiasm a sense of ownership usually generates. And the specific task is to tap the right sort of community involvement: ways have to be found to empower specific groups of people who can play a more positive role in making sure benefits go to those who need it most. For example, bringing all child development and educational programs under the purview of the *panchayat*, and building in some form of collective responsibility and performance-based grants to *panchayat*s, may be just the sort of group/community incentive that creates more enthusiasm for health, child development and education programs at the local level. However, there is a relevant issue to be dealt with here: to what extent are the *panchayat*s or local bodies representative of the larger community? Also to be emphasized is the learning from various programs across sectors that *while quality assurance can be an outcome of community involvement, the perceived quality of a provision is an important factor in mobilizing community involvement.* Thus the greater involvement of parents and the community needs to be proactively sought so that responsibility can be shared at local levels, and quality as defined by the child's

---

[111]Ramachandran et al 2003.

community can be ensured. A case in point is the well-known Tamil Nadu School Meal Program, which rests on the strength of community participation. To build up to the point of genuine public involvement in the development of the child, such a range of links must be forged across the spectrum of Indian society.

Using information, education and communication to involve the community:

The research review makes it clear that society at large, and the child's immediate community in particular, must be harnessed to support child development and ensure that services are appropriately delivered. In other words, *the immediate community must become the principal, informed "spokesperson" of the child and the nurturer and protector of the child's rights. How is this to happen? By using information in a planned and organized fashion, to educate and communicate.* The first critical use of information lies in promoting awareness. The qualitative case studies found that general awareness about nutrition was low, while there was better awareness about the importance of education.[112] This implies that policies and programs need integrated, focused communication strategies to increase awareness – for example about the harmful effects of deliberately eating less during pregnancy; or the vital link between the child's future development on the one hand, and on the other, pre-school education, immunization, Vitamin A supplementation, and external nutrition for the growing child.

Public education is particularly important, for instance, to link complete immunization with disease prevention and the transmission of communicable diseases. It can forge, in the public mind, the relationship between proper sanitation, safe water storage and dispensing practices, and disease prevalence.

We also have examples of experiences to indicate how IEC can be used effectively. The DPEP has used folk media, *jathas*[113] and *ma-beti melas*[114] in an effective way in, for example, promoting the participation of girls in primary education. In an example of convergent action, DPEP, the *Mahila Samakhya Program*[115] and UNICEF have made use of a character called *Meena* to communicate several social messages regarding nutrition and education. These campaigns are in several languages and make effective use of multimedia. The *Meena* campaign of the UNICEF has had a good result across sectors, particularly in areas like gender discrimination. The need for such interventions is made sharper by the IEC issue of a frequent case of "disconnect" – bombarding the large population of illiterates in the targeted community with text based messages. The only way to make IEC effective is to adapt it to the local context of needs.

Thus, if used in a contextualized way, IEC can comprise indispensable means to change behavior, and it needs more resources and better management. Hence this report recommends that IEC be built into projects to formulate messages using a

---

[112]Ibid.

[113]Public, "on-the-street" campaigns.

[114] Literally, "mother-daughter" fairs; public campaign for girls and women.

[115]The program provides valuable support to the DPEP.

client-oriented approach. Outreach workers need training in interpersonal communication and counseling, in carefully researching campaigns, and in monitoring impact.[116]

It may also be worthwhile to revisit earlier nutrition education and preventive health programs and strengthen their IEC components. One of the lessons learnt from these programs was the need to front-load IEC in any program, using local media rather than materials that mean time-consuming procurement and development. This will provide adequate time for attitudinal change and, consequently, better utilization and monitoring by the community of the program interventions. Another learning has been the need for greater focus on direct community contact through the use of direct campaigns, folk media, multimedia and endorsement by popular and well-known figures in the community, as is being done in the polio campaign.

Creating awareness of facts and issues also means promoting the environment for debate and dialogue. This would mean that the community evolves into that necessary spokesperson for the child by debating, for instance, what a good quality life is, in their children's context. Such debate would also mean more realistic and rooted assessments of certain problems that have got trapped in a vicious cycle of deprivation (poverty) leading to more deprivation (being out of school). Perhaps one of the best examples of an area where more such debate is required, not just at the policy and project design

level, but also at the community level, is that of child labor and schooling. A more intensive debate across the board, taking into account current evidence on child work, may yield facts and perspectives that can be fed back into the making of appropriate policies and programs for these most vulnerable of children.

Investing in the very young child on a priority basis:

We have said time and again that any planning for children must address the entire child development continuum from prenatal-11+ years. But the review also indicates the need for a special focus on the early years in terms of planning as well as resource allocation. The research clearly shows the strong and positive impact of ECCE on enrollment, attendance and retention outcomes – all of which lead to the Millennium Development Goal of successful primary completion. Placing a priority on greater investment in the early years and on expanding access to quality ECD provisions is expected to reduce child mortality, reduce malnutrition, and most of all, improve children's life chances.

We have already seen that ECD programs can contribute to better nutrition and health, and better rates of school enrollment.[117] A study of about 33,000 children across eight Indian states shows that ECD has a significant impact (15-20 percent) on retention in primary grades.[118] With such an increase in pre-school attendance and retention rates, the

---

[116]World Bank 1999c

[117]Myers 1995.

[118]Kaul et al 1993.

cumulative impact of ECD on completion rates is likely to be significant.

If ECD is so clearly a priority area, the next question relates to spending on this fundamental aspect of the Indian child's development. Unfortunately, the analysis of research clearly shows that we are not spending enough on the young child. A comparative analysis of trends in per child expenditure for ICDS and Elementary Education (which are taken as proxy for expenditures on children below 6 years and from 6-14 years respectively) indicates the expenditure on the older age group to be significantly higher than for the younger age group, across all states. This becomes a matter of great concern. *While global research indicates that 85 percent of a child's core brain structure is already formed by age three, so that investing in the early years is critical, the trend indicates that actual spending per child on children below 6 years is almost one-eighth of the spending on children in the 6-14 age group, across all states indicating a gross neglect of the foundation years of childhood. (See Figure 6.4).*

With constant scarcity of resources, the general tendency among planners and policy makers is to argue that funds cannot be "diverted" to the below-primary age- group when "we do not have enough to universalize primary education." This report emphasizes the conclusion that this is a misplaced priority given the above rationale and the growing evidence across the globe that early interventions are both crucial and cost-effective. In the Brazilian PROAPE project, the total costs of schooling, including the early learning program itself, for pupils up-to grade 2 of primary education was 11 percent lower for those who participated in the

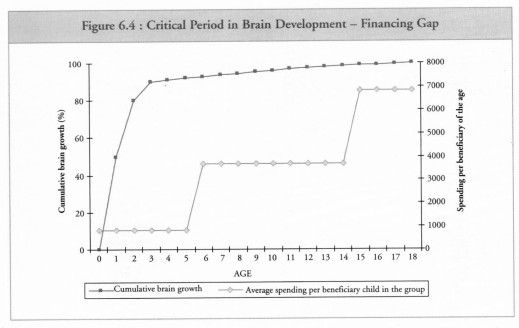

Figure 6.4 : Critical Period in Brain Development – Financing Gap

Source: Karoly et al. 1998

ECCD as compared to those who did not. It would be useful to carry out a similar study in India to elicit empirical evidence on the cost effectiveness of investments in early childhood interventions in the context of not only the expected outcomes but also the cost effectiveness of subsequent investments. *Given the existing global evidence, this research makes a strong recommendation for increasing spending on the early childhood stage for children below 6 years, on a priority basis alongside for primary education, nutrition and health of 6-14 year olds, to ensure both immediate and long term gains.*

Targeting public financing for poor children:

A close examination of trends in public expenditure on children has revealed that less than two percent of the overall GOI budget is aimed at children. Though total government spending on children has gone up by more than eight times during the nineties, the increase is smaller in real terms. Indeed, it would be correct to say the increase has been marginal. And of this increase, the largest slice is that on education and somewhat for health, while that for nutrition and early childhood development is insignificant, indicating a clear imbalance. If we consider trends in state spending, while increases are there, the major bulk of these go towards payment of salaries and other operational expenses, thus leaving very little for components that will really make a difference to the child. In view of the perpetual shortfall of funds and

the Indian child's increasingly urgent needs, the funds for children are, simply, inadequate. Furthermore, there are large-scale interstate variations in spending on the social sector. and more particularly on children (See Figure 6.5 as indicative from the ICDS budget). The states with the poorest CDI status, such as Bihar and Uttar Pradesh, also appear to spend less per child on major centrally sponsored programs. Also, these states in which the need for resources is greater also have a wider resource gap, if the per child estimations of the Planning commission for ICDS were compared with actual allocations. A possible factor determining allocations could be the limited implementation capacity of the state. This interdependence of resources and implementation capacity very likely creates a vicious cycle of low resources, weak capacity and poor development, which is difficult to break in many states in India.

(Refer Fig.5.3) A recent finding raises the possibility that increased public spending has a stronger impact on child development outcomes in the poor states as opposed to those in non-poor states.[119] If this is so, the unit cost of improving child development indicators in the poor states would be much lower than that in the more advanced states. A possible explanation offered by the study is that in the poor states, "the sheer inadequacy of health and school services and infrastructure is so great that there is substantial scope for reducing infant mortality or

Two significant policy decisions would make programs based on the new policy paradigm possible: a) "virtual" pooling of resources for children across sectors (and ministries) and a b) bottom-up planning process based on Village Plans for Children prepared at the community level.

---

[119]Deolalikar 2003.

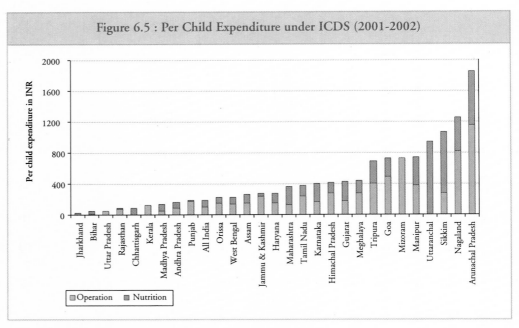

Figure 6.5 : Per Child Expenditure under ICDS (2001-2002)

Source: Planning Commission, GOI 2002b.

increasing enrollments via simple, low-cost interventions." What is clear enough though is that the greater challenge in these states makes a strong case for better targeting of poorer states, while all the way pushing for more efficient spending.

The Tenth Five Year Plan acknowledges that one of the lessons learnt from the experiences of implementing the Ninth Five Year Plan was that *addressing "the whole child" is more cost-effective than individual services delivered separately. Thus, the Report makes a strong case for child-based budgeting using a bottom-up approach.* Such an approach would use per child cost vis-à-vis the expected interventions at each sub-stage as the unit of costing, as opposed to schematic, norm-based budgeting. This is consistent with the idea of decentralized planning and the preparation of comprehensive village plans for children. The children's needs would get distributed at the district, state and national levels in a matrix form across sectors – in terms of mapped priorities – and, accordingly, inform program budgets.

Given the limited resources available with the government and its track record of service delivery, the question arises – to what extent and where should government at the Federal and provincial levels, put to use its limited resources, so that the returns are significant. The World Development Report (2003) provides a framework for thinking through this question. Inferring from this Framework, there is no ambiguity in that the government will have to be the dominant provider for children's development and education due to the pro-poor focus, heterogeneous nature of interventions and complexity of monitoring of provisions related to children. *However, considerations of equity and efficiency* coupled with the constraints of limited resources and the need for maximizing welfare impact, call for a rational targeting of public resources for the poorest of the poor; alongside this, efforts would also are required to mobilize/encourage private investment through a policy based on combination of incentives and regulation, so as to enable wider access. Possibilities of cost sharing and pooling of resources by multiple stakeholders in support of a common framework could also be a way forward to ensure wider coverage and better quality. In addition to enhanced funding through multiple sources, the study also recommends *the need for governance and administrative reforms and greater focus in all projects on strengthening institutional capacity, which would enable the money allocated to be spent with greater accountability, greater focus on outcomes, and most of all, with less risk of perpetuating inequities.*

The Way Ahead : Changing the Policy Paradigm for Child-Related Interventions

Moving towards an outcome-focused and child-centered approach to planning for children: using successful completion of primary school as marker for integrated child development; locating planning and monitoring of programs within holistic framework; targeting total context of child within and outside family; responding to intersecting needs of women and children; converging child development programs with programs for women's literacy.

Moving from a sectoral to a multi-sectoral approach: mapping priorities across current sectors/ schemes; DWCD taking greater responsibility for crèches and play centers for prenatal-3 year-olds, and DOE, the same for ECE for 3-6 year olds.

Moving from a supply-driven to a demand-driven, business plan approach: more demand-based, bottom-up approach that reflects community needs and priorities.

Moving from centralised and standardized planning to contextualized, convergent and decentralized planning: preparing multi-sectoral Village Plans for Children that draw on existing schemes across sectors to focus on the specific and contextual needs of children across health, nutrition and education sectors, and along childhood development continuum using an area-intensive approach at decentralized levels. Setting up of National Advisory Group for Child Development to identify specific areas with potential for convergence at the national and sub-national levels and inform central planning consistent with conceptual framework; decentralizing to the level of local management, involving and empowering PRIs with built-in accountability and incentives; building capacity for context-specific solutions; community consultation;

Moving towards better targeting and closer monitoring: scaling up interventions to reach ST and SC children, girls, poor and rural children, children in the northern and western states; close attention to data use and quality; sensitization to relevant issues to change attitudes and enhance community-level capacity.

The Way Ahead : Changing the Policy Paradigm for Child-Related Interventions (Contd.)

Moving towards better service delivery: further analysis of access and quality; thorough review of systems; more flexible spending linked to specific needs of area and target populations; governance issues – decentralization of planning and management, supported by devolution of autonomy and finance, capacity building of local management institutions; bringing all child development and educational programs under purview of panchayat; building in collective responsibility and performance-based grants; clarification and rationalization of roles at the grassroots level, particularly in ICDS.

Making the private sector more accountable and forging new partnership: bringing more accountability in the private sector provisions through community awareness and forging new institutional arrangements and partnerships.

Moving towards better use of information to mobilize the community: build IEC into projects to formulate messages using a client-oriented approach; train outreach workers in interpersonal communication, counseling, campaign research, monitoring impact; integrated, focused communication strategies to increase awareness; revisit earlier nutrition education and preventive health programs and strengthen IEC components; front-load IEC in terms of time frame to provide adequate time for attitudinal change, better utilization and monitoring; greater focus on direct community contact.

Moving towards greater investment in the very young child on a priority basis: greater investment in and expanding access to quality ECCE provisions.

Moving towards targeting public financing for poor children: better targeting of public resources to poorer states and poorest communities; mobilizing private investment to widen access through incentives and regulation.

▬ Appendix

Members of the Technical Committee and Core Committee

Dr. R.V.V. Ayyar, Secretary,
Department of Women and Child Development,
Government of India.

Ms. Prema Ramachandran,
Advisor (Health),
Planning Commission,
Government of India.

Mr. Sumit Bose, Joint Secretary,
Department of Elementary Education
& Literacy,
Ministry of Human Resource Development,
Government of India.

Dr. Rekha Bhargava, Joint Secretary,
Department of Women and Child Development,
Government of India.

Ms. Rashmi Sharma, Director EEC,
Department of Education,
Government of India.

Ms. Shalini Prasad, Director EEB,
Department of Education,
Government of India.

Dr. S. Sarkar, Deputy Commissioner (Child Health),
Ministry of Health and Family Welfare,
Government of India.

Mina Swaminathan,
M.S. Swaminathan Research Foundation,
Chennai.

Dr. Ramji,
Department of Pediatrics (Neonatology),
All India Institute of Medical Sciences, New Delhi.

Dr. Geeta Sodhi,
Swasthya,
New Delhi.

Mr. Amarjeet Sinha,
Education Advisor,
DFID, New Delhi.

Ms. Patrice Engle,
Chief Nutrition/Child Development, UNICEF,
New Delhi.

Ms. Deepika Shrivastava, Project Officer,
Nutrition/Child Development, UNICEF,
New Delhi.

Dr. Neerja Sharma,
Department of Child Development,
Lady Irwin College,
New Delhi.

Dr. Adarsh Sharma,
National Institute of Public Cooperation &
Child Development,
New Delhi.

Dr. D.B. Gupta,
National Council of Applied Economic Research,
New Delhi.

Dr. Sharda Jain, Director,
"Sandhan",
Jaipur.

Dr. Pratibha Singhi,
Department of Paediatrics,
Post Graduate Institute of Medical Sciences,
Chandigarh.

Ms. Zakiya Kurien, Director,
Center for Learning Resources,
Pune.

Ms. Shahnaz Wazir, Senior Research officer,
National Institute of Nutrition,
Jamia Osmania,
Hyderabad.

Ms. K. Lakshmi,
Andhra Mahila Sabha,
Hyderabad.

≡ Bibliography

Anandalakshmi, S. 1982. "Cognitive Competence in Infancy." Unpublished. Department of Child Development, Lady Irwin College, University of Delhi.

Basu, D.D. 1994. *Shorter Constitution of India.* 11th edition, New Delhi: Prentice-Hall of India Pvt. Ltd.

Bhattacharya, A. K. 1981. "Nutritional Deprivation and Related Emotional Aspects in *Calcutta Children." Child Abuse and Neglect* 5(4): 467-474.

Bloom, B.S. 1964. *Stability and Change in Human Characteristics.* New York: John Wiley and Sons.

Choksi, Armeane, In Foreword to Mary Young, *Early Childhood Development: Investing in the Future,* World Bank, Washington, D.C., 1996.

Consultative Group on Early Childhood Care and Development. 2000. *Early Childhood Counts.* Published by the World Bank on behalf of Consultative Group.

Deolalikar, Anil. 2003. "Attaining the Millennium Development Goals in India: How Likely and What Will it Take?" Unpublished draft. Human Development Sector, South Asia Region, World Bank.

Doherty, Gillian. 1997. Zero to Six: The Basis for School Readiness. Applied Research Branch R-97-8E, Ottawa: Human Resources Development Canada.

Duraiswamy, P. 2000. "Changes to Return in Education in India, 1983-94, by Gender, Age Cohort and Location." Working Paper No. 815. Economic Growth Center, Yale University.

Fuller, B. and P. Clarke. 1994. "Raising School Effects and Ignoring Culture? Local Conditions and the Influence of the Classroom Tools, Rules and Pedagogy." Review of Educational Research (64).

Ghai, O. P. 1975. "Effect of Marasmic Malnutrition on Subsequent Mental Development." India Paediatrics, Journal of Indian Paediatrics 12.

Goel, Suparva. 1993. "Nutritional Problems in India." Health and Population: Perspectives and Issues 16.

Government of India (GOI). 1996a. Annual Report 1995-96, Department of Women and Child Development, New Delhi.

GOI 1996b. Communication For Behavior Change Action Plan-ICDS II. Unpublished, Department of Women and Child Development, New Delhi.

GOI 1997. Annual Report 1996-97, Department of Women and Child Development, New Delhi.

GOI 2001. Annual Report 2000-01 Department of Women and Child Development, New Delhi.

GOI 1998a. National Consultation on Control Of Nutritional Anemia in India. Ministry of Health and Family Welfare, New Delhi.

GOI 1998b. Annual Report 1997-98, Department of Education, Ministry of Human Resources Development, New Delhi.

GOI 1999a. Note on ICDS Program. Unpublished. Department of Women and Child Development, New Delhi.

GOI 1999b. Annual Report 1998-99, Department of Women and Child Development, New Delhi.

GOI 2001a. Annual Report 2000-01, Department of Women and Child Development, New Delhi.

GOI 2001b. Census of India 2001. Series 29- Andhra

Pradesh. Paper 1 of 2001, Provisional Population Totals. Hyderabad: Director of Census Operations.

GOI 2001c. Census of India 2001. Series 29- Andhra Pradesh. Paper 2 of 2001, Rural-Urban Distribution of Population. Director of Census Operations, Hyderabad.

GOI 2001d. Midterm Review of the Ninth Five-Year Plan. Planning Commission, New Delhi.

GOI 2001e. Census of India. Paper 1 of 2001, Provisional Population Totals. Registrar General and Census Commissioner, India, New Delhi.

GOI 2001f. Select Education Statistics as of September 1999. Department of Education, Ministry of Health and Human Resources Development, New Delhi.

GOI 2001g. Report of the Working Group on Health Care and Children for the Tenth Plan. Planning Commission, New Delhi.

GOI 2001h. Report of the Working Group on Child Development for the Tenth Plan. Planning Commission, New Delhi.

GOI 2001i. "Health, Nutrition and Family Welfare Program: Review of Progress during the Ninth Plan Period." Working Paper Series, No. 1/2001-PC. Planning Commission, New Delhi.

GOI 2001j. Convention on the Rights of the Child, India. First Periodic Report. New Delhi: Department of Women and Child Development.

GOI 2001k. Annual Report, Department of Education, New Delhi.

GOI 2002a. Report of the Steering Committee on Family Welfare. Planning Commission, New Delhi.

GOI 2002b. Annual Plans for States, Planning Commission, New Delhi.

GOI 2003a. Tenth Five Year Plan Working Group Report. Planning Commission, New Delhi.

GOI 2003b. Review of the Ninth Five Year Plan, Working Group on Child Development for the Tenth Five Year Plan, Department of Women and Child Development, New Delhi.

GOI Expenditure Budget. I, II. Demand for Grants for various years including Budget Statements of Department of Women and Child Development, Department of Health, Department of Family Welfare, Department of Elementary Education and Literacy, Ministry of Labor; and Law and Justice, Ministry of Law, Justice and Company Affairs.

Gupta, Devendra B. 2003a. "Study of the Existing Policies and Related Provisions/Schemes Promoting the Developmental and Educational Needs of Children in the Age Group 0-11 Years." Study commissioned by the World Bank, New Delhi.

Gupta, Devendra B. 2003b. "Public Spending on Child Development." Study commissioned by the World Bank, New Delhi.

HAQ: Center for Child Rights. 2001. "India's Children and the Union Budget." Study by HAQ, New Delhi, supported by Save the Children.

Heckman, James and Carnerio, Pedro. 2003. "Human Capital Policy" National Bureau of Economic Research: Working Paper. Cambridge, U.K.

Heneveld, Ward. 1999. In T. S. Saraswathi, ed., 1999. Culture, Socialization and Human Development: Theory, Research and Application in India. New Delhi: Sage Publications.

Heywood, Peter. 2003. "ICDS Survey Results: Program Implications." Midterm Review, Shimla.

Indicus Analytics. 2003. "Empirical Analysis of the Conceptual Framework for Integrated Child Development." Study commissioned by the World Bank, New Delhi.

International Institute For Population Sciences (IIPS). 1993. National Family Health Survey (NFHS I). International Institute for Population Sciences, Mumbai.

(IIPS) 1995. India: National Family Health Survey, 1992-93. International Institute for Population Sciences, Mumbai.

(IIPS) 2000a. Reproductive and Child Health Project, Rapid Household Survey, India (1998). Mumbai: International Institute for Population Sciences.

(IIPS) 2000b. India, National Family Health Survey (NFHS-2), 1998-99. International Institute for Population Sciences, Mumbai.

Jandhyala, Kameshwari. In Ramachandran, Vimala. 2002. Hierarchies of Access – Gender and Social Equity in Primary Education. New Delhi: European Commission.

Jha, J. and Jhingran, D. 2002. "Elementary Education for the Poorest and Other Deprived Groups: The Real Challenge of Universalization." New Delhi: Center for Policy Research.

Karoly, L. A. et al. Investing in Our Children. RAND, 1998

Kaul, V. 1989, 1992. Seminar Reports., Unpublished National Council for Educational Research and Training, New Delhi.

Kaul, V., C. Ramachandran and G. C. Upadhayay. 1994. Impact of ECE on Retention in Primary Grades, A Longitudinal Study. New Delhi: National Council for Educational Research and Training.

Kaul, V. et al. 1996. "Process-Based Readiness Program for Primary Level Mathematics – A Longitudinal Study" In Indian Educational Review. New Delhi: National Council for Educational Research and Training.

Kaul, V. and Ramachandran, C. 1999. "Parental Child Rearing Practices and School Achievement." Unpublished research study.

Kaul, V. 2000. "National Program of Nutritional Support to Primary Education in India." In Neera Ramachandran and Lionel Massum (eds.), Coming to Grips with Rural Child Work: A Food Security Approach. World Food Program and Institute of Human Development, New Delhi: Manohar Publishers.

Kaul, V. et al. 2003. A study on Shikan Puthi: A DPEP experiment in Self Learning , Axom Sarva Shiksha Abhiyan Mission, Assam.

Levinger, B. 1994, Del Rosso and Marek 1996. Early Childhood Care and Education in the Context of Education for All. Cited in New Concept Information Systems, 2002.

Lockheed, M. and Verspoor, A. 1991. Improving Primary Education in Developing Countries. New York: Oxford University Press.

Lozoff, B. (1990). "Has iron deficiency been shown to cause altered behavior in infants?" In J. Dobbing (ed.), Brain, Behavior, and Iron in the Infant Diet. London: Springer-Verlag.

Martorell et al. 1995. "Guatemala -- The Benefits of ECD Programs: An Economic Analysis." Education, Annexure 2, p. 5. World Bank, Washington, D.C.

Martorell, Reynaldo, 1997. "Under-nutrition during Pregnancy and Early Childhood: Consequences for Cognitive and Behavior Development." In Mary E. Young (ed.) Early Childhood Development: Investing In Our Children's Future, World Bank, Elsevier, 1997.

McCain, Margaret N., and J. Fraser Mustard. 1999. Reversing the Real Brain Drain. Early Years Study, The Founder's Network, Ontario,Canada.

Mooij, Jos and Mahendra Dev. 2002. "Social Sector Priorities: An Analysis of Budgets and Expenditures in India in the 1990s." IDS Working Paper 164, Sussex.

Myers, Robert G. 1992. "The Impact of Health and Nutrition on Education." World Bank Research Observer 2(1), 1996.

Myers, Robert G. 1995. The Twelve Who Survive: Strengthening Programs of Early Childhood Development in the Third World. 2nd edition. Ypsilanti, Michigan: High Scope Press.

Natesan, H. and Devdas, R.P. 1981. Measurement of Mental Abilities of Well Nourished and Malnourished Children. Journal of Psychological Researches 25(3).

National Council for Applied Economic Research (NCAER). 1999. "Accessibility and Attainment in Education and Health Care." MARGIN 31.

NCAER 1999a. Integrated Child Development Services. Field Survey, New Delhi.

NCAER 1999b. India Human Development Report. Delhi: Oxford University Press.

NCAER 1995. Primary Education in the Web of Poverty Culture. School Effectiveness and Learning Achievement at Primary Stage. New Delhi: National Council for Educational Research and Training.

NCAER 1996. Pre-school Education: Challenges and Opportunities 1993. Sixth Educational Survey. New Delhi: National Council for Educational Research and Training.

NCAER 1997. The Primary Years: Towards a Curriculum Framework. New Delhi: Departments of Pre-school and Primary Education, National Council for Educational Research and Training.

NCAER 1998. The Primary Years: Towards a Curriculum 8–11. New Delhi: National Council for Educational Research and Training

NCAER 2001. National Curriculum of Elementary and Secondary Education. New Delhi: National Council for Educational Research and Training.

New Concept Information Systems Pvt. Ltd., New Delhi. 2003. "Integrated Child Development – A Conceptual Framework." Study commissioned by the World Bank, New Delhi.

NSSO (National Sample Survey Organization). 1996. data, 52nd Round. New Delhi: Ministry of Planning, Department of Statistics.

NSSO data, 55th Round Employment Survey (1999-2000).

Operations Research Group. 1994 and 1996. Evaluation of Non-Formal Education Program in Lok Jumbish project. New Delhi.

ORG 1999. "Evaluation Study to Assess the Efficiency and Effectiveness of the National Program for Nutritional Support to Primary Education in Ten States of India." Report submitted to UNICEF, New Delhi.

Panda, P. et al. 1993. "Health Status of Under-Fives in Ludhiana Slum." Health and Population: Perspectives and Issues 16(3, 4).

Peters, David et al. 2002. Better Health Systems for India's Poor: Findings, Analysis, and Options. Health, Nutrition and Population Series, Human Development Network. Washington, D. C.: World Bank.

PROBE Survey Report. 1999. Public Report on Basic Education in India. Oxford University Press New Delhi.

Ramachandran, Vimala. 2002. Hierarchies of Access: Gender and Social Equity in Primary Education. European Commission: New Delhi.

Ramachandran, Vimala. 2003a. "Backward and Forward Linkages that Strengthen Primary Education." Economic and Political Weekly, 8 March 2003.

Ramachandran, Vimala. (ed.), 2003b Getting Children Back to School – Case Studies in Primary Education. New Delhi: Sage Publications.

Ramachandran, Vimala et. al. 2003. Snakes and Ladders: Factors that Facilitate/Impede Successful Primary School Completion. Educational Resource Unit, New Delhi. Study commissioned by the World Bank, New Delhi.

Ranjan, J. and Krishnamachari K. A. V. R.. 1997. "Community-Based Strategy for Improved Health Care Delivery in the Agency Areas: Case Study of ITDA Rampachodavaram." Presented at the seminar on Perspectives and Strategies for Sustainable Tribal Development Beyond 2000 AD, April 29-30, 1997. Department of Anthropology, Andhra University, Vishakapatnam.

Sen, Amartya. 1999. Development as Freedom. New York: Knopf.

Shore R. 1997. "Rethinking the Brain," New York Families and Work Institute.

Sternberg, R. J., & Grigorenko, E. L. (1997). Interventions for cognitive development in children 0-3 years old. In M. Young (Ed.), Early child development: Investing in our children's future (pp. 127-156). Amsterdam: Elsevier.

Swaminathan, M. 1990. "The First Three Years: A Sourcebook on Early Childhood Care and Education." Report.

Swaminathan, M. 2000. "Quality Matters." M.S. Swaminathan Research Foundation (MSSRF), Chennai.

UNESCO/OECD. 2002. Financing Education – Investments and Returns, Analysis of the World Education Indicators. Paris.

UNICEF. 1994, 1996, 1997, 1998, 1999, 2000 and 2003. The State of the World's Children. Geneva.

UNICEF. Facilitators' Resource Guide. Video 1: Off To A Good Start. UNICEF : New Delhi.

UNICEF and Department of Women and Child Development. 2001. Multiple Indicator Survey – Andhra Pradesh. Draft. New Delhi: UNICEF.

Upadhyaya, G.C. et al (1998). Numeracy and Reading Readiness Levels of Entrants to Class 1—A Synthesis Report. National Council for Educational Research and Training, New Delhi.

World Health Organization. 1999. A Critical Link: Interventions for Physical Growth and Psychological Development.

World Bank. 1995. Priorities and Strategies for Education: A World Bank Review. Washington, D. C.: World Bank.

World Bank. 1996. Primary Education In India. Development in Practice. Delhi: World Bank and Allied Publishers

World Bank. 1997a. Primary Education in India. Delhi: World Bank and Allied Publishers

World Bank. 1997b. Primary Education in India. Delhi: World Bank and Allied Publishers.

World Bank. 1998a. "India Wasting Away. The Crises of Malnutrition in India." Health, Nutrition and Population Unit, South Asia Region, New Delhi.

World Bank. 1998b. Parenting in the Early Years: A Review of Programs for Parents of Children from Birth to Three Years. Washington, D. C.: World Bank.

World Bank. 1999a. The Ten Who Go To School: School Health and Nutrition Programming in Latin America and the Caribbean. Washington, D. C.: World Bank.

World Bank. 1999b. A Food Supplementation Program in India. Health Care: Case Studies.

World Bank. 1999c. Health Care in India: Learning from Experience. OED (187).

World Bank. 2000. "Reaching Out to the Child." Report of a Workshop in Child Development, New Delhi, South Asia Education Sector Technical Working Paper 1.

World Bank. 2001. Development of the Child: A Multi-sectoral Perspective. Unpublished.

World Bank. 2003. "A Review of Educational Progress and Reform in the DPEP (Phases I and II)." Human Development Sector, South Asia Region, New Delhi.

World Bank. 2003. "World Development Indicators." Development Data Group.

World Bank. 2004. "World Development Report"

Young, Mary. E. 1996. Early Child Development: Investing in the Future, Washington, D. C.: World Bank.

Young, Mary.et al. 1997. Early Child Development: Investing in our Children's Future. Proceedings of a World Bank conference on Early Child Development entitled "Investing in the Future," Atlanta, Georgia, 1996. World Bank, Washington, D. C.